How People Learn

BRIDGING
RESEARCH
AND
PRACTICE

M. Suzanne Donovan, John D. Bransford, and James W. Pellegrino, *editors*

Committee on Learning Research and Educational Practice

Commission on Behavioral and Social Sciences and Education

National Research Council

NATIONAL ACADEMY PRESS
Washington, DC

NATIONAL ACADEMY PRESS • 2101 Constitution Avenue, NW • Washington, DC 20418

NOTICE: The project that is the subject of this report was approved by the Governing Board of the National Research Council, whose members are drawn from the councils of the National Academy of Sciences, the National Academy of Engineering, and the Institute of Medicine. The members of the committee responsible for the report were chosen for their special competences and with regard for appropriate balance.

The National Academy of Sciences is a private, nonprofit, self-perpetuating society of distinguished scholars engaged in scientific and engineering research, dedicated to the further-ance of science and technology and to their use for the general welfare. Upon the authority of the charter granted to it by the Congress in 1863, the Academy has a mandate that requires it to advise the federal government on scientific and technical matters. Dr. Bruce M. Alberts is president of the National Academy of Sciences.

The National Academy of Engineering was established in 1964, under the charter of the National Academy of Sciences, as a parallel organization of outstanding engineers. It is autono-mous in its administration and in the selection of its members, sharing with the National Acad-emy of Sciences the responsibility for advising the federal government. The National Academy of Engineering also sponsors engineering programs aimed at meeting national needs, encour-ages education and research, and recognizes the superior achievements of engineers. Dr. William A. Wulf is president of the National Academy of Engineering.

The Institute of Medicine was established in 1970 by the National Academy of Sciences to secure the services of eminent members of appropriate professions in the examination of policy matters pertaining to the health of the public. The Institute acts under the responsibility given to the National Academy of Sciences by its congressional charter to be an adviser to the federal government and, upon its own initiative, to identify issues of medical care, research, and education. Dr. Kenneth I. Shine is president of the Institute of Medicine.

The National Research Council was organized by the National Academy of Sciences in 1916 to associate the broad community of science and technology with the Academy's pur-poses of furthering knowledge and advising the federal government. Functioning in accor-dance with general policies determined by the Academy, the Council has become the principal operating agency of both the National Academy of Sciences and the National Academy of Engineering in providing services to the government, the public, and the scientific and engi-neering communities. The Council is administered jointly by both Academies and the Institute of Medicine. Dr. Bruce M. Alberts and Dr. William A. Wulf are chairman and vice chairman, respectively, of the National Research Council.

The study was supported by Grant No. R215U980027 between the National Academy of Sciences and the U.S. Department of Education. Any opinions, findings, conclusions, or recom-mendations expressed in this publication are those of the author(s) and do not necessarily reflect the view of the organizations or agencies that provided support for this project.

International Standard Book Number 0-309-06536-4

Additional copies of this report are available from: National Academy Press, 2101 Constitution Avenue N.W. Lockbox 285, Washington, D.C. 20055
Call 800-624-6242 or 202-334-3313 (in the Washington Metropolitan Area).

This report is also available online at **http://www.nap.edu**

First Printing, June 1999   **Seventh Printing, February 2003**
Second Printing, October 1999   **Eighth Printing, November 2003**
Third Printing, March 2000   **Ninth Printing, September 2004**
Fourth Printing, November 2000   **Tenth Printing, September 2005**
Fifth Printing, July 2001   **Eleventh Printing, August 2006**
Sixth Printing, August 2002

COMMITTEE ON LEARNING RESEARCH AND EDUCATIONAL PRACTICE

Acknowledgments

The inspiration for this project was Alexandra Wigdor, director of the Division on Education, Labor, and Human Performance at the National Research Council (NRC). Her leadership in guiding the formation and work of the Committee on Learning Research and Educational Practice was central to its success. The vision of focusing the efforts of the research community on classroom practice is that of C. Kent McGuire, assistant secretary for educational research and improvement at the U.S. Department of Education. Our point of departure for this project was the National Research Council report *How People Learn: Brain, Mind, Experience, and School.* We acknowledge the contribution of the Committee on Developments in the Science of Learning who authored that report: John Bransford (co-chair), Ann Brown (co-chair), John Anderson, Rochel Gelman, Robert Glaser, William Greenough, Gloria Ladson-Billings, Barbara Means, Jose Mestre, Linda Nathan, Roy Pea, Penelope Peterson, Barbara Rogoff, Thomas Romberg, and Samuel Wineberg. Without their work, ours would not have been possible. Rodney Cocking, study director of that committee, provided support for this committee's efforts to carry that report one step further. Wendell Grant, the project assistant, worked long hours managing the logistics of the committee's meetings and events, and providing the administrative support for production of the report and its drafts. Christine McShane improved the document with her skilled editing. We also thank Carolyn Stalcup for design support and Sandra Yurchak for secretarial support.

The committee held a conference in December 1998 to present *How People Learn* to an audience of educators, policy makers, and researchers and to elicit their feedback on the promise of, and obstacles to, bridging educational research and practice. The National Research Council and the Office of Educational Research and Improvement (OERI) of the U.S. Department of Education cosponsored the conference, and the participation of

Bruce Alberts, NRC chair, and C. Kent McGuire, assistant secretary for OERI, contributed to its success. Joseph Conaty and Luna Levinson of OERI assisted with conference planning. Karen Fuson, committee member Annemarie Palincsar, and Robert Bain demonstrated approaches to teaching that use the principles highlighted in this report. Members of the two panels provided insightful perspectives on the challenge of bridging research and classroom practice: on the panel providing teacher perspectives were: David Berliner, Deanna Burney, Janice Jackson, Jean Krusi, Lucy (Mahon) West, and Robert Morse. On the panel providing policy perspectives were: Ron Cowell, Louis Gomez, Paul Goren, Jack Jennings, Kerri Mazzoni, and Carol Stewart.

The committee also held a workshop to focus more sharply on the research that would help construct the bridge between research and practice. The workshop was an intensive two-day effort to work in both large and small groups to cover each of the areas of research discussed in this report. We thank each of the participants who joined the committee in this effort: Amy Alvarado, Karen Bachofer, Robert Bain, Cathy Cerveny, Cathy Colglazier, Rodney Cocking, Ron Cowell, Jean Krusi, Luna Levinson, Robert Morse, Barbara Scott Nelson, Iris Rotberg, Leona Schauble, Carol Stewart, and Lucy West for their diligent efforts.

This report has been reviewed in draft form by individuals chosen for their diverse perspectives and technical expertise, in accordance with procedures approved by the NRC's Report Review Committee. The purpose of this independent review is to provide candid and critical comments that will assist the institution in making the published report as sound as possible and to ensure that the report meets institutional standards for objectivity, evidence, and responsiveness to the study charge. The review comments and draft manuscript remain confidential to protect the integrity of the deliberative process.

We thank the following individuals for their participation in the review of this report: Dorothy Fowler, Lacey Instructional Center, Annandale, VA; Ramesh Gangolli, Department of Mathematics, University of Washington; Richard Lehrer, Department of Educational Psychology, University of Wisconsin-Madison; Michael Martinez, Education Department, University of California, Irvine; K. Ann Renninger, Program in Education, Swarthmore College; Thomas A. Romberg, National Center for Research in Mathematical Sciences Education, University of Wisconsin-Madison; and Patrick Suppes, Center for the Study of Language and Information, Stanford University.

Although the individuals listed above have provided constructive comments and suggestions, it must be emphasized that responsibility for the final content of this report rests entirely with the authoring committee and the institution.

John Bransford, Co-chair
James Pellegrino, Co-chair
Suzanne Donovan, Study Director
Committee on Learning Research
and Educational Practice

Contents

Summary

In December 1998, the National Research Council released *How People Learn*, a report that synthesizes research on human learning. The research put forward in the report has important implications for how our society educates: for the design of curricula, instruction, assessments, and learning environments. The U.S. Department of Education's Office of Educational Research and Improvement (OERI), which funded *How People Learn*, has posed the next question: What research and development could help incorporate the insights from the report into classroom practice? Responding to that question is the focus of this report.

To address OERI's question, the Committee on Learning Research and Educational Practice first considered how research and practice are generally linked. A small number of teachers are engaged in design experiments with researchers or explore research on their own. They constitute a direct link between research and practice. But for the most part, the influence of research on practice is filtered through educational materials, through pre-service and in-service teacher education, through public policy, and through public opinion—often gleaned from mass media reporting and from people's own experiences in schools.

The committee sees the influence of research on these mediating arenas as weak. The research base on learning and teaching has not been consolidated in a way that gives consistent, clear messages in formats that are useful for practice. As a result, the various mediating arenas that influence practice are often not aligned either with research findings or with each other. In synthesizing a broad body of research, *How People Learn* provides an opportunity to provide research-based messages that are clear and directly relevant to classroom practice. Three of the findings are highlighted in this report because they have both a solid research base to support them and strong implications for how the enterprise of education is conducted:

- Students come to the classroom with preconceptions about how the world works. If their initial understanding is not engaged, they may fail to grasp new concepts and information presented in the classroom, or they may learn them for purposes of a test but revert to their preconceptions outside the classroom. This finding requires that teachers be prepared to draw out their students' existing understandings and help to shape them into an understanding that reflects the concepts and knowledge in the particular discipline of study.

- To develop competence in an area of learning, students must have both a deep foundation of factual knowledge and a strong conceptual framework. Research that compares the performance of novices and experts, as well as research on learning and transfer, shows clearly that experts are not just "smart people"; they also draw on a richly structured information base. But this factual information is not enough. Key to expertise is the mastery of concepts that allow for deep understanding of that information, transforming it from a set of facts into usable knowledge. The conceptual framework allows experts to organize information into meaningful patterns and store it hierarchically in memory to facilitate retrieval for problem solving. And unlike pure acquisition of factual knowledge, the mastery of concepts facilitates transfer of learning to new problems. This research has clear implications for what is taught, how it is taught, and the preparation required for teaching.

- Strategies can be taught that allow students to monitor their understanding and progress in problem solving. Research on the performance of experts reveals that they monitor their understanding carefully, making note of when additional information is required, whether new information is consistent with what is already known, and what analogies can be drawn that would advance their understanding. In problem solving, they consider alternatives and are mindful of whether the one chosen is leading to the desired end. Although this monitoring goes on as an internal conversation, the strategies involved are part of a culture of inquiry, and they can be successfully taught in the context of subject matter. In teaching them, the monitoring questions and observations are modeled and discussed for some time in the classroom, with the ultimate goal of independent monitoring and learning. This research, again, has clear implications for teacher preparation, as well as for curriculum design.

To explore how these insights from research might be incorporated into practice, the committee convened both a conference and a workshop. Both events brought together teachers, administrators, researchers, curriculum specialists, and education policy makers. The conference solicited feedback on *How People Learn*, its potential to influence classroom practice, and the barriers to its doing so. The workshop focused more specifically on research and development that could help bridge research and practice. This report incorporates the many insights of participants. From these, the committee drew five overarching goals that helped to guide the design of the research agenda that is the heart of this report:

- Elaborate the messages in *How People Learn* at a level of detail that makes them usable to educators (including teacher educators) and policy makers.
- Communicate the messages in *How People Learn* in a manner that is effective for each of the audiences that influences educational practice.
- Use the principles of learning for understanding articulated in *How People Learn* as a lens through which to evaluate existing education practices (K-12 and teacher training programs) and policies.
- Conduct research in teams that combine the expertise of researchers and the wisdom of practitioners.
- Extend the frontier of learning research through more intensive study of classroom practice.

In the research and development agenda proposed here, these goals are incorporated into a comprehensive program of "use-inspired" strategic research and development focused on issues of improving classroom learning and teaching. The research and development proposed addresses needs in each of the four mediating arenas. With respect to educational materials, the proposals include a review of a sample of existing curricula, with the goal of identifying areas of alignment with the principles of learning that might be replicated or built on. Research and development are also recommended to extend the existing knowledge base by developing and testing new educational materials and by elaborating key research findings from *How People Learn*. Finally, creating an electronic database for information on curricula that have been evaluated by a team of experts is proposed.

The principles of learning highlighted here apply to teacher education and professional development programs as well as to K-12 education. The committee proposes that current practices in schools of education and professional development programs be evaluated for alignment with the principles of learning. The development and study of new tools for teacher training are proposed, as is an elaboration of key findings from *How People Learn* as they apply to teacher learning.

In the area of public policy, research is proposed to review state standards and assessments through the lens of *How People Learn.* Research to extend the knowledge base by studying district-level reform efforts that have been successful is proposed as well. And the development and study of effective communication tools for policy makers are recommended. Similarly, the development of a popular version of *How People Learn* is suggested in order to promote an understanding among parents and the public of the principles of learning that it identifies, as well as their implications for classroom practice.

Although much can be done now with the research reviewed in *How People Learn,* many unanswered research questions with clear importance for classroom practice remain. The committee therefore recommends research that would extend the knowledge base in areas in which it is now weak.

Finally, the committee suggests experimentation with, and study of, an interactive communications site where information and research findings from these proposed efforts can be accessed by a variety of audiences. The goal of this effort is to provide a knowledge base that is useful to teachers and to the various mediating groups that contribute to educational practice.

1

Introduction

The quest to understand human learning has, in the past four decades, undergone dramatic change. Once a matter for philosophical argument, the workings of the mind and the brain are now subject to powerful research tools. From that research, a science of learning is emerging.

In 1995, the U.S. Department of Education's Office of Educational Research and Improvement (OERI) requested that the National Research Council (NRC) synthesize research on the science of learning. The resulting report, *How People Learn*, reviews research literature on human learning and suggests important implications for the design of curricula, instruction, assessments, and learning environments (National Research Council, 1999a). It suggests further that many existing school practices are inconsistent with what is known about effective learning.

The purpose of this report is to ask how the insights from the research reviewed in *How People Learn* can be incorporated into classroom practice and to suggest a research and development agenda that would inform and stimulate the required change. The implications of the report for educational practice and its determinants are fundamental and far-reaching. Still, there are many influences on classroom practice that are unrelated to the research reviewed in *How People Learn*. We know, for example, that nutrition affects ability to learn. The adequacy and safety of the school can have direct influences on learning. An alternative salary structure for the teaching profession can affect the ability of schools to attract and keep qualified teachers, which in turn influences learning. We exclude these many issues here, not as a judgment regarding their significance, but because they fall outside the charge of the committee. Our focus is on the issues for which learning research gives guidance.

FRAMING THE AGENDA

As a first step in framing a research and development agenda, the committee considered what would be required for insights from research to be integrated into classroom practice. The influence of research on educational practice has been weak for a variety of reasons. Educators generally do not look to research for guidance. The concern of researchers for the validity and robustness of their work, as well as their focus on underlying constructs that explain learning, often differ from the focus of educators on the applicability of those constructs in real classroom settings with many students, restricted time, and a variety of demands. Even the language used by researchers is very different from that familiar to teachers. And the full schedules of many teachers leaves them with little time to identify and read relevant research. These factors contribute to the feeling voiced by many teachers that research has largely been irrelevant to their work (Fleming, 1988).

Despite these formidable barriers, past research has at times managed to influence practice, albeit slowly and for the most part indirectly. The paths of influence, as the committee sees them, are illustrated in Figure 1.1. To a limited extent, research directly influences classroom practice when teachers and researchers collaborate in design experiments, or when interested teachers incorporate ideas from research into their classroom practice. This appears as the only line directly linking research and practice in Figure 1.1. More typically, ideas from research are filtered through the development of education materials, through pre-service and in-service teacher and administrator education programs, through public policies at the national, state, and school district level, and through the public's beliefs about learning and teaching, often gleaned from the popular media and from their own experiences in school. These are the four arenas that mediate the link between research and practice in Figure 1.1. The public includes teachers, whose beliefs may be influenced by popular presentations of research, and parents, whose beliefs about learning and teaching affect classroom practice as well.

Teachers are the key to change in this model; they are the classroom practitioners. Many excellent teachers already incorporate the principles in *How People Learn* into their practice, either by design or by intuition. But for those principles to be used systematically, all teachers will need opportunities to understand the principles, be persuaded of their usefulness, and be able to enact them in their classrooms. The principals who evaluate the teachers and who provide leadership in defining the schools' goals will need to be persuaded of their value as well. To achieve that goal, teacher educa-

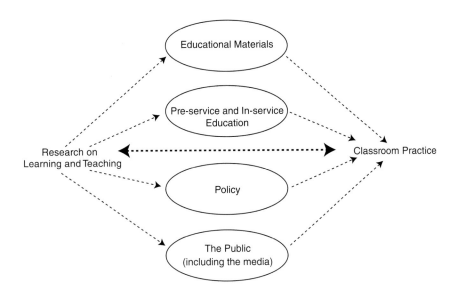

FIGURE 1.1 *Paths through which research influences practice.*

tion and professional development programs for both teachers and administrators will need to incorporate the principles of learning.

Teachers work with teaching tools. They are unlikely to change their practice significantly in the absence of supporting curricular materials. Those who develop curricula and companion guides, software, instructional techniques, and assessments will therefore need to understand and incorporate the principles of learning into their products if teachers are to successfully change their practice.

But change at the classroom level can be supported or thwarted by public policy. For the principles in *How People Learn* to affect practice, district-level school boards and administrators must be persuaded of the value of that change, and must lend it legitimacy and support. Policy makers at the national and state levels will also need to understand those principles and to set policies that are consistent with them. Otherwise, teacher efforts can be undermined by standards, assessments, and teaching and textbook requirements. Moreover, the level of funding allocated to activities required for change can facilitate or debilitate the effort.

Finally, teachers, administrators, and policy makers are ultimately accountable to parents and to other stakeholders in the business community and the public. Their understanding of and support for change can be a force for advancement or resistance.

In Figure 1.1, broken rather than solid lines are used to connect research on learning to the four mediating arenas; they illustrate weak lines of influence. Because they are weak, there is often a lack of alignment among them. Consequently, teachers frequently struggle to adapt to competing demands. Strategies for change are often short-lived and responsive to fads rather than to sound research and theory.

In synthesizing a broad body of research, *How People Learn* provides an opportunity to strengthen the messages of research for the communities who contribute to education practice. It identifies key principles of learning that do have a firm scientific basis. It represents a beginning attempt to provide foundational knowledge that could be used to strengthen the links between research and the mediating arenas, providing a common set of assumptions about learning that could promote greater alignment among those arenas. Although the principles of learning will continue to be tested and elaborated, they will not be tomorrow's castaway fads.

How People Learn is most usefully viewed, *not* as a set of answers, but as the basis for a conversation among researchers and practitioners about the kinds of knowledge, tools, and resources that would promote student learning and achievement. That is how the committee has used the report. It has been the basis for conversations between committee members and those involved in education practice and policy.

Those conversations were held at two events. The first was a conference at which the findings of *How People Learn* were presented to an audience of over 150 researchers, educators, administrators, curriculum developers, and policy makers. Researchers and teachers who work on the development of curricula and instructional techniques presented teaching demonstrations that incorporate the principles in *How People Learn*. Panels of educators and policy makers provided comments on the report's findings, the potential of those findings to influence practice, and perceived barriers to change. They also offered ideas for addressing those barriers.

At a subsequent workshop, a smaller group of 25 convened to consider more specifically the research and development that might bring the insights from *How People Learn* into classrooms. Groups of teachers, teacher educators, researchers, and policy makers made specific suggestions to the committee. Those suggestions influenced the committee's work significantly.

The contributions of participants at both the workshop and the conference are incorporated throughout this report.

PLAN OF THE REPORT

Following this introduction, Chapter 2 summarizes some of the key findings from *How People Learn* and outlines implications of those findings for teaching and for designing classroom environments. *How People Learn* is a lengthy report that covers a large field of research. Our effort here is not to summarize the entire document, but to focus on those findings and messages that are most directly relevant to classroom practice and to the mediating arenas that influence it.

Chapter 3 summarizes responses from educators and policy makers that were offered at the conference and at the workshop. More specific suggestions made by workshop participants regarding research and development are incorporated into Chapter 4, in which the committee presents its recommendations for a research and development agenda. The agenda is organized around each of the mediating arenas outlined above: educational materials, pre-service and in-service education, public policy, and public opinion and the media. In it the committee considers the research and development that would link each arena with the findings in *How People Learn*. The committee further recommends research that would extend the knowledge base reviewed in *How People Learn* in ways that directly support the goal of effective education.

2

Key Findings

How People Learn provides a broad overview of research on learners and learning and on teachers and teaching. Three of those findings are highlighted here because they have both a solid research base to support them and strong implications for how we teach. It is not the committee's intention to suggest that these are the only insights from research that can beneficially be incorporated into practice. Indeed, a number of additional findings are discussed in *How People Learn*.

1. Students come to the classroom with preconceptions about how the world works. If their initial understanding is not engaged, they may fail to grasp the new concepts and information that are taught, or they may learn them for purposes of a test but revert to their preconceptions outside the classroom.

Research on early learning suggests that the process of making sense of the world begins at a very young age. Children begin in preschool years to develop sophisticated understandings (whether accurate or not) of the phenomena around them (Wellman, 1990). Those initial understandings can have a powerful effect on the integration of new concepts and information. Sometimes those understandings are accurate, providing a foundation for building new knowledge. But sometimes they are inaccurate (Carey and Gelman, 1991). In science, students often have misconceptions of physical properties that cannot be easily observed. In humanities, their preconceptions often include stereotypes or simplifications, as when history is understood as a struggle between good guys and bad guys (Gardner, 1991). A critical feature of effective teaching is that it elicits from students their preexisting understanding of the subject matter to be taught and provides opportunities to build on—or challenge—the initial understanding. James

Minstrell, a high school physics teacher, describes the process as follows (Minstrell, 1989: 130-131):

> Students' initial ideas about mechanics are like strands of yarn, some unconnected, some loosely interwoven. The act of instruction can be viewed as helping the students unravel individual strands of belief, label them, and then weave them into a fabric of more complete understanding. Rather than denying the relevancy of a belief, teachers might do better by helping students differentiate their present ideas from and integrate them into conceptual beliefs more like those of scientists.

The understandings that children bring to the classroom can already be quite powerful in the early grades. For example, some children have been found to hold onto their preconception of a flat earth by imagining a round earth to be shaped like a pancake (Vosniadou and Brewer, 1989). This construction of a new understanding is guided by a model of the earth that helps the child explain how people can stand or walk on its surface. Many young children have trouble giving up the notion that one-eighth is greater than one-fourth, because 8 is more than 4 (Gelman and Gallistel, 1978). If children were blank slates, telling them that the earth is round or that one-fourth is greater than one-eighth would be adequate. But since they already have ideas about the earth and about numbers, those ideas must be directly addressed in order to transform or expand them.

Drawing out and working with existing understandings is important for learners of all ages. Numerous research experiments demonstrate the persistence of preexisting understandings among older students even after a new model has been taught that contradicts the naïve understanding. For example, in a study of physics students from elite, technologically oriented colleges, Andrea DiSessa (1982) instructed them to play a computerized game that required them to direct a computer-simulated object called a dynaturtle so that it would hit a target and do so with minimum speed at impact. Participants were introduced to the game and given a hands-on trial that allowed them to apply a few taps with a small wooden mallet to a tennis ball on a table before beginning the game. The same game was also played by elementary schoolchildren. DiSessa found that both groups of students failed dismally. Success would have required demonstrating an understanding of Newton's laws of motion. Despite their training, college physics students, like the elementary schoolchildren, aimed the moving dynaturtle directly at the target, failing to take momentum into account. Further investigation of one college student who participated in the study revealed that she knew the relevant physical properties and formulas, yet, in the context of the game, she fell back on her untrained conception of how the physical world works.

Students at a variety of ages persist in their beliefs that seasons are caused by the earth's distance from the sun rather than by the tilt of the earth (Harvard-Smithsonian Center for Astrophysics, 1987), or that an object that had been tossed in the air has both the force of gravity and the force of the hand that tossed it acting on it, despite training to the contrary (Clement, 1982). For the scientific understanding to replace the naïve understanding, students must reveal the latter and have the opportunity to see where it falls short.

2. To develop competence in an area of inquiry, students must: (a) have a deep foundation of factual knowledge, (b) understand facts and ideas in the context of a conceptual framework, and (c) organize knowledge in ways that facilitate retrieval and application.

This principle emerges from research that compares the performance of experts and novices and from research on learning and transfer. Experts, regardless of the field, always draw on a richly structured information base; they are not just "good thinkers" or "smart people." The ability to plan a task, to notice patterns, to generate reasonable arguments and explanations, and to draw analogies to other problems are all more closely intertwined with factual knowledge than was once believed.

But knowledge of a large set of disconnected facts is not sufficient. To develop competence in an area of inquiry, students must have opportunities to learn with understanding. Deep understanding of subject matter transforms factual information into usable knowledge. A pronounced difference between experts and novices is that experts' command of concepts shapes their understanding of new information: it allows them to see patterns, relationships, or discrepancies that are not apparent to novices. They do not necessarily have better overall memories than other people. But their conceptual understanding allows them to extract a level of meaning from information that is not apparent to novices, and this helps them select and remember relevant information. Experts are also able to fluently access relevant knowledge because their understanding of subject matter allows them to quickly identify what is relevant. Hence, their attention is not over-taxed by complex events.

In most areas of study in K-12 education, students will begin as novices; they will have informal ideas about the subject of study, and will vary in the amount of information they have acquired. The enterprise of education can be viewed as moving students in the direction of more formal understanding (or greater expertise). This will require both a deepening of the information base and the development of a conceptual framework for that subject matter.

Geography can be used to illustrate the manner in which expertise is organized around principles that support understanding. A student can learn to fill in a map by memorizing states, cities, countries, etc., and can complete the task with a high level of accuracy. But if the boundaries are removed, the problem becomes much more difficult. There are no concepts supporting the student's information. An expert who understands that borders often developed because natural phenomena (like mountains or water bodies) separated people, and that large cities often arose in locations that allowed for trade (along rivers, large lakes, and at coastal ports) will easily outperform the novice. The more developed the conceptual understanding of the needs of cities and the resource base that drew people to them, the more meaningful the map becomes. Students can become more expert if the geographical information they are taught is placed in the appropriate conceptual framework.

A key finding in the learning and transfer literature is that organizing information into a conceptual framework allows for greater "transfer"; that is, it allows the student to apply what was learned in new situations and to learn related information more quickly (see Box 2.1). The student who has learned geographical information for the Americas in a conceptual framework approaches the task of learning the geography of another part of the globe with questions, ideas, and expectations that help guide acquisition of the new information. Understanding the geographical importance of the Mississippi River sets the stage for the student's understanding of the geographical importance of the Nile. And as concepts are reinforced, the student will transfer learning beyond the classroom, observing and inquiring, for example, about the geographic features of a visited city that help explain its location and size (Holyoak, 1984; Novick and Holyoak, 1991).

3. A "metacognitive" approach to instruction can help students learn to take control of their own learning by defining learning goals and monitoring their progress in achieving them.

In research with experts who were asked to verbalize their thinking as they worked, it was revealed that they monitored their own understanding carefully, making note of when additional information was required for understanding, whether new information was consistent with what they already

BOX 2.1   Throwing Darts Under Water

In one of the most famous early studies comparing the effects of learning a procedure with learning with understanding, two groups of children practiced throwing darts at a target under water (described in Judd, 1908; see a conceptual replication by Hendrickson and Schroeder, 1941). One group received an explanation of the refraction of light, which causes the apparent location of the target to be deceptive. The other group only practiced dart throwing, without the explanation. Both groups did equally well on the practice task, which involved a target 12 inches under water. But the group that had been instructed about the abstract principle did much better when they had to transfer to a situation in which the target was under only 4 inches of water. Because they understood what they were doing, the group that had received instruction about the refraction of light could adjust their behavior to the new task.

knew, and what analogies could be drawn that would advance their understanding. These meta-cognitive monitoring activities are an important component of what is called adaptive expertise (Hatano, 1990).

Because metacognition often takes the form of an internal conversation, it can easily be assumed that individuals will develop the internal dialogue on their own. Yet many of the strategies we use for thinking reflect cultural norms and methods of inquiry (Hutchins, 1995; Brice-Heath, 1981, 1983; Suina and Smolkin, 1994). Research has demonstrated that children can be taught these strategies, including the ability to predict outcomes, explain to oneself in order to improve understanding, note failures to comprehend, activate background knowledge, plan ahead, and apportion time and memory. Reciprocal teaching, for example, is a technique designed to improve students' reading comprehension by helping them explicate, elaborate, and monitor their understanding as they read (Palincsar and Brown, 1982). The model for using the meta-cognitive strategies is provided initially by the teacher, and students practice and discuss the strategies as they learn to use them. Ultimately, students are able to prompt themselves and monitor their own comprehension without teacher support.

The teaching of metacognitive activities must be incorporated into the subject matter that students are learning (White and Frederickson, 1998). These strategies are not generic across subjects, and attempts to teach them as generic can lead to failure to transfer. Teaching metacognitive strategies in context has been shown to improve understanding in physics (White and Frederickson, 1998), written composition (Scardamalia et al., 1984), and heuristic methods for mathematical problem solving (Schoenfeld, 1983, 1984, 1991). And metacognitive practices have been shown to increase the degree to which students transfer to new settings and events (Lin and Lehman, in press; Palincsar and Brown, 1982; Scardamalia et al., 1984; Schoenfeld, 1983, 1984, 1991).

Each of these techniques shares a strategy of teaching and modeling the process of generating alternative approaches (to developing an idea in writing or a strategy for problem solving in mathematics), evaluating their merits in helping to attain a goal, and monitoring progress toward that goal. Class discussions are used to support skill development, with a goal of independence and self-regulation.

IMPLICATIONS FOR TEACHING

The three core learning principles described above, simple though they seem, have profound implications for the enterprise of teaching and teacher preparation.

1. *Teachers must draw out and work with the preexisting understandings that their students bring with them.* This requires that:

- The model of the child as an empty vessel to be filled with knowledge provided by the teacher must be replaced. Instead, the teacher must actively inquire into students' thinking, creating classroom tasks and conditions under which student thinking can be revealed. Students' initial conceptions then provide the foundation on which the more formal understanding of the subject matter is built.

- The roles for assessment must be expanded beyond the traditional concept of testing. The use of frequent formative assessment helps make students' thinking visible to themselves, their peers, and their teacher. This provides feedback that can guide modification and refinement in thinking. Given the goal of learning with understanding, assessments must tap understanding rather than merely the ability to repeat facts or perform isolated skills.

• Schools of education must provide beginning teachers with opportunities to learn: (a) to recognize predictable preconceptions of students that make the mastery of particular subject matter challenging, (b) to draw out preconceptions that are not predictable, and (c) to work with preconceptions so that children build on them, challenge them and, when appropriate, replace them.

2. Teachers must teach some subject matter in depth, providing many examples in which the same concept is at work and providing a firm foundation of factual knowledge. This requires that:

• Superficial coverage of all topics in a subject area must be replaced with in-depth coverage of fewer topics that allows key concepts in that discipline to be understood. The goal of coverage need not be abandoned entirely, of course. But there must be a sufficient number of cases of in-depth study to allow students to grasp the defining concepts in specific domains within a discipline. Moreover, in-depth study in a domain often requires that ideas be carried beyond a single school year before students can make the transition from informal to formal ideas. This will require active coordination of the curriculum across school years.

• Teachers must come to teaching with the experience of in-depth study of the subject area themselves. Before a teacher can develop powerful pedagogical tools, he or she must be familiar with the progress of inquiry and the terms of discourse in the discipline, as well as understand the relationship between information and the concepts that help organize that information in the discipline. But equally important, the teacher must have a grasp of the growth and development of students' thinking about these concepts. The latter will be essential to developing teaching expertise, but not expertise in the discipline. It may therefore require courses, or course supplements, that are designed specifically for teachers.

• Assessment for purposes of accountability (e.g., statewide assessments) must test deep understanding rather than surface knowledge. Assessment tools are often the standard by which teachers are held accountable. A teacher is put in a bind if she or he is asked to teach for deep conceptual understanding, but in doing so produces students who perform more poorly on standardized tests. Unless new assessment tools are aligned with new approaches to teaching, the latter are unlikely to muster support among the schools and their constituent parents. This goal is as important as it is difficult to achieve. The format of standardized tests can encourage measurement of factual knowledge rather than conceptual understanding, but it also facilitates objective scoring.   Measuring depth of understanding can pose challenges for objectivity.   Much work needs to be done to minimize the trade-off between assessing depth and assessing objectively.

3. *The teaching of metacognitive skills should be integrated into the curriculum in a variety of subject areas.* Because metacognition often takes the form of an internal dialogue, many students may be unaware of its importance unless the processes are explicitly emphasized by teachers. An emphasis on metacognition needs to accompany instruction in each of the disciplines, because the type of monitoring required will vary. In history, for example, the student might be asking himself, "who wrote this document, and how does that affect the interpretation of events," whereas in physics the student might be monitoring her understanding of the underlying physical principle at work.

*   Integration of metacognitive instruction with discipline-based learning can enhance student achievement and develop in students the ability to learn independently. It should be consciously incorporated into curricula across disciplines and age levels.
*   Developing strong metacognitive strategies and learning to teach those strategies in a classroom environment should be standard features of the curriculum in schools of education.

Evidence from research indicates that when these three principles are incorporated into teaching, student achievement improves.   For example, the Thinker Tools Curriculum for teaching physics in an interactive computer environment focuses on fundamental physical concepts and properties, allowing students to test their preconceptions in model building and experimentation activities. The program includes an "inquiry cycle" that helps students monitor where they are in the inquiry process. The program asks for students' reflective assessments and allows them to review the assessments of their fellow students. In one study, sixth graders in a suburban school who were taught physics using Thinker Tools performed better at solving conceptual physics problems than did eleventh and twelfth grade physics students in the same school system taught by conventional methods. A second study comparing urban students in grades 7 to 9 with suburban students in grades 11 and 12 again showed that the younger students taught by the inquiry-based approach had a superior grasp of the fundamental principles of physics (White and Frederickson, 1997, 1998).

BRINGING ORDER TO CHAOS

A benefit of focusing on how people learn is that it helps bring order to a seeming cacophony of choices. Consider the many possible teaching strategies that are debated in education circles and the media. Figure 2.1 depicts them in diagram format: lecture-based teaching, text-based teaching, inquiry-based teaching, technology-enhanced teaching, teaching organized around individuals versus cooperative groups, and so forth. Are some of these teaching techniques better than others? Is lecturing a poor way to teach, as many seem to claim? Is cooperative learning effective? Do attempts to use computers (technology-enhanced teaching) help achievement or hurt it?

How People Learn suggests that these are the wrong questions. Asking which teaching technique is best is analogous to asking which tool is best—a hammer, a screwdriver, a knife, or pliers. In teaching as in carpentry, the selection of tools depends on the task at hand and the materials one is

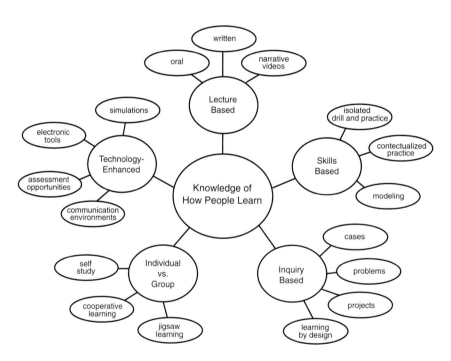

FIGURE 2.1 *With knowledge of how people learn, teachers can choose more purposefully among techniques to accomplish specific goals.*

working with. Books and lectures *can* be wonderfully efficient modes of transmitting new information for learning, exciting the imagination, and honing students' critical faculties—but one would choose other kinds of activities to elicit from students their preconceptions and level of understanding, or to help them see the power of using meta-cognitive strategies to monitor their learning. Hands-on experiments *can* be a powerful way to ground emergent knowledge, but they do not alone evoke the underlying conceptual understandings that aid generalization. There is no universal best teaching practice.

If, instead, the point of departure is a core set of learning principles, then the selection of teaching strategies (mediated, of course, by subject matter, grade level, and desired outcome) can be purposeful. The many possibilities then become a rich set of opportunities from which a teacher constructs an instructional program rather than a chaos of competing alternatives.

Focusing on how people learn also will help teachers move beyond either-or dichotomies that have plagued the field of education. One such issue is whether schools should emphasize "the basics" or teach thinking and problem-solving skills. *How People Learn* shows that both are necessary.   Students' abilities to acquire organized sets of facts and skills are actually enhanced when they are connected to meaningful problem-solving activities, and when students are helped to understand why, when, and how those facts and skills are relevant. And attempts to teach thinking skills without a strong base of factual knowledge do not promote problem-solving ability or support transfer to new situations.

DESIGNING CLASSROOM ENVIRONMENTS

How People Learn proposes a framework to help guide the design and evaluation of environments that can optimize learning (Figure 2.2). Drawing heavily on the three principles discussed above, it posits four inter-related attributes of learning environments that need cultivation.

1. *Schools and classrooms must be learner centered.* Teachers must pay close attention to the knowledge, skills, and attitudes that learners bring into the classroom. This incorporates the preconceptions regarding subject matter already discussed, but it also includes a broader understanding of the learner. For example:
- Cultural differences can affect students' comfort level in working collaboratively versus individually, and they are reflected in the background knowledge students bring to a new learning situation (Moll et al., 1993).

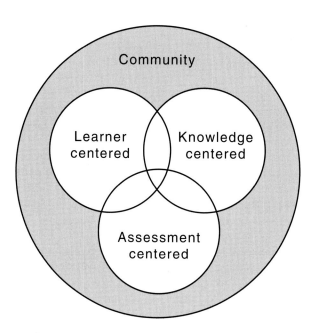

FIGURE 2.2 *Design of learning environments.*

• Students' theories of what it means to be intelligent can affect their performance. Research shows that students who think that intelligence is a fixed entity are more likely to be performance oriented than learning oriented—they want to look good rather than risk making mistakes while learning. These students are especially likely to bail out when tasks become difficult. In contrast, students who think that intelligence is malleable are more willing to struggle with challenging tasks; they are more comfortable with risk (Dweck, 1989; Dweck and Legget, 1988).

Teachers in learner-centered classrooms also pay close attention to the individual progress of each student and devise tasks that are appropriate. Learner-centered teachers present students with "just manageable difficulties"—that is, challenging enough to maintain engagement, but not so difficult as to lead to discouragement. They must therefore have an understanding of their students' knowledge, skill levels, and interests (Duckworth, 1987).

2. *To provide a knowledge-centered classroom environment, attention must be given to what is taught (information, subject matter), why it is taught (understanding), and what competence or mastery looks like.* As mentioned above, research discussed in *How People Learn* shows clearly that expertise involves well-organized knowledge that supports understanding, and that learning with understanding is important for the development of expertise because it makes new learning easier (i.e., supports transfer).

Learning with understanding is often harder to accomplish than simply memorizing, and it takes more time. Many curricula fail to support learning with understanding because they present too many disconnected facts in too short a time—the "mile wide, inch deep" problem. Tests often reinforce memorizing rather than understanding. The knowledge-centered environment provides the necessary depth of study, assessing student understanding rather than factual memory. It incorporates the teaching of meta-cognitive strategies that further facilitate future learning.

Knowledge-centered environments also look beyond engagement as the primary index of successful teaching (Prawaf et al., 1992). Students' interest or engagement in a task is clearly important. Nevertheless, it does not guarantee that students will acquire the kinds of knowledge that will support new learning. There are important differences between tasks and projects that encourage hands-on doing and those that encourage doing with understanding; the knowledge-centered environment emphasizes the latter (Greeno, 1991).

3. *Formative assessments—ongoing assessments designed to make students' thinking visible to both teachers and students—are essential. They permit the teacher to grasp the students' preconceptions, understand where the students are in the "developmental corridor" from informal to formal thinking, and design instruction accordingly. In the assessment-centered classroom environment, formative assessments help both teachers and students monitor progress.*

An important feature of assessments in these classrooms is that they be learner-friendly: they are not the Friday quiz for which information is memorized the night before, and for which the student is given a grade that ranks him or her with respect to classmates. Rather, these assessments should provide students with opportunities to revise and improve their thinking (Vye et al., 1998b), help students see their own progress over the course of weeks or months, and help teachers identify problems that need to be remedied (problems that may not be visible without the assessments). For example, a high school class studying the principles of democracy might be given a scenario in which a colony of people have just settled on the moon and must establish a government. Proposals from students of the defining features of such a government, as well as discussion of the problems they foresee in its establishment, can reveal to both teachers and students areas in which student thinking is more and less advanced. The exercise is less a test than an indicator of where inquiry and instruction should focus.

4. *Learning is influenced in fundamental ways by the context in which it takes place. A community-centered approach requires the development of norms for the classroom and school, as well as connections to the outside world, that support core learning values.*

The norms established in the classroom have strong effects on students' achievement. In some schools, the norms could be expressed as "don't get caught not knowing something." Others encourage academic risk-taking and opportunities to make mistakes, obtain feedback, and revise. Clearly, if students are to reveal their preconceptions about a subject matter, their questions, and their progress toward understanding, the norms of the school must support their doing so.

Teachers must attend to designing classroom activities and helping students organize their work in ways that promote the kind of intellectual camaraderie and the attitudes toward learning that build a sense of community. In such a community, students might help one another solve problems by building on each other's knowledge, asking questions to clarify explanations, and suggesting avenues that would move the group toward its goal (Brown and Campione, 1994). Both cooperation in problem solving (Evans, 1989; Newstead and Evans, 1995) and argumentation (Goldman, 1994; Habermas, 1990; Kuhn, 1991; Moshman, 1995a, 1995b; Salmon and Zeitz, 1995; Youniss and Damon, 1992) among students in such an intellectual community enhance cognitive development.

Teachers must be enabled and encouraged to establish a community of learners among themselves (Lave and Wegner, 1991). These communities can build a sense of comfort with questioning rather than knowing the answer and can develop a model of creating new ideas that build on the contributions of individual members. They can engender a sense of the excitement of learning that is then transferred to the classroom, conferring a sense of ownership of new ideas as they apply to theory and practice.

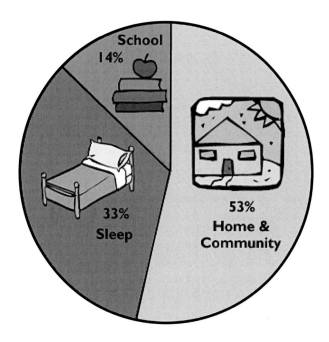

FIGURE 2.3 *Students spend only 14 percent of their time in school.*

Not least, schools need to develop ways to link classroom learning to other aspects of students' lives. Engendering parent support for the core learning principles and parent involvement in the learning process is of utmost importance (Moll, 1990; 1986a, 1986b). Figure 2.3 shows the percentage of time, during a calendar year, that students in a large school district spent in school. If one-third of their time outside school (not counting sleeping) is spent watching television, then students apparently spend more hours per year watching television than attending school. A focus only on the hours that students currently spend in school overlooks the many opportunities for guided learning in other settings.

APPLYING THE DESIGN FRAMEWORK TO ADULT LEARNING

The design framework above assumes that the learners are children, but the principles apply to adult learning as well. This point is particularly important because incorporating the principles in *How People Learn* into educational practice will require a good deal of adult learning. Many approaches to teaching adults consistently violate principles for optimizing learning. Professional development programs for teachers, for example, frequently:

- *Are not learner centered.* Rather than ask teachers where they need help, they are simply expected to attend prearranged workshops.
- *Are not knowledge centered.* Teachers may simply be introduced to a new technique (like cooperative learning) without being given the opportunity to understand why, when, where, and how it might be valuable to them. Especially important is the need to integrate the structure of activities with the content of the curriculum that is taught.
- *Are not assessment centered.* In order for teachers to change their practices, they need opportunities to try things out in their classrooms and then receive feedback. Most professional development opportunities do not provide such feedback. Moreover, they tend to focus on change in teaching practice as the goal, but they neglect to develop in teachers the capacity to judge successful transfer of the technique to the classroom or its effects on student achievement.
- *Are not community centered.* Many professional development opportunities are conducted in isolation. Opportunities for continued contact and support as teachers incorporate new ideas into their teaching are limited, yet the rapid spread of Internet access provides a ready means of maintaining such contact if appropriately designed tools and services are available.

The principles of learning and their implications for designing learning environments apply equally to child and adult learning. They provide a lens through which current practice can be viewed with respect to K-12 teaching *and* with respect to preparation of teachers in the research and development agenda. The principles are relevant as well when we consider other groups, such as policy makers and the public, whose learning is also required for educational practice to change.

3

Responses from the Education and Policy Communities

The Committee on Learning Research and Educational Practice invited members of the teacher, administrator, policy, and research communities to come together for the purpose of providing feedback on *How People Learn* and discussing ideas regarding the potential for, and the barriers to, bridging research and practice. The December 1998 conference provided exposure to the report and an opportunity for panel members, as well as members of a diverse audience, to comment. The smaller January 1999 workshop provided the opportunity for groups of teachers, education administrators and policy makers, teacher educators, and researchers to suggest ideas regarding the research and development that is required to link the findings in *How People Learn* to classroom practice. They also noted areas in which additional research on learning is required. In what follows, we highlight many of the responses the committee heard. More specific ideas regarding research and development are incorporated into the agenda in Chapter 4.

RESPONSES FROM THE EDUCATION COMMUNITY

The teachers involved in the conference and workshop came from schools that were both urban and suburban, public and private. They serve children from a variety of socioeconomic backgrounds (see Appendix A for the list of participants). Collectively, they represent vast experience in teaching, and some now serve, or have served in the past, as school administrators. They uniformly agreed that *How People Learn* provides knowledge that is important and relevant for classroom teaching and that is not now reflected in most teaching practice. But they also agreed that it was only a start. They provided a number of suggestions for next steps.

- **Research findings need to be organized and communicated to teachers and other educators in a way that is easy to comprehend and to integrate into their current thinking.** To accomplish this, the language and examples used in communicating research ideas must be familiar.
- **The model of how people learn needs to be presented as a standard, stable model** that rests on solid research that will not alter dramatically in the 5 or 10 years it will take to implement. The report, *How People Learn,* is seen as a start in the direction of building such a model of human learning. But more needs to be done. The model needs to make sense of areas in which current practice is effective, it must ring true to the everyday experience of teachers, and it must suggest changes to current practice that is ineffective. It must allow practitioners to use the model to guide solutions to their problems, not merely to explain successes after they occur.
- **Teachers need curriculum materials and support to adopt new teaching methods.** A clear discussion of how people learn will not be adequate to influence teacher practice. Teachers need the research to be elaborated in the form of many examples that are relevant to their own teaching and in the form of curricula that they can use in their classrooms. There is consensus among many of the educators that simply providing a curriculum, however exemplary, is not enough. Teachers need visual models of practice, and support over an extended period of time as they attempt to use the curriculum. They need to have questions answered, and they need feedback when what they observe is different from what they expect.
- **Collaboration between teachers and researchers will require a change in the relationship between the two groups.** To achieve more fluid communication between those who teach and those who do research, a level of trust must be in place that does not currently exist. Teachers often feel that researchers are unaware of the realities of classroom teaching, and that research does not address the questions that they need to have answered. If teachers are to buy into research-based changes in teaching, they must be part of a collaborative effort that makes use of their knowledge and insights and that responds to their needs. If they are invested in a research effort from the beginning, they will be more open to its results.
- **Teachers need time and incentives to reflect on their practice, as well as opportunities to use that time to learn about new research**

and curricula. There appears to be widespread consensus among educators that time limitations are an enormous barrier to bridging research and practice. Teachers' days are so tightly scheduled that they barely have adequate time to think about their lessons for the next day. Many have too little time to reflect on their own practice and to engage in reflective dialogue with their colleagues. Fewer still have the additional time and motivation to investigate relevant research. If that is to change, time outside the classroom needs to be scheduled into a teachers' work week and work year.

   • **For teachers to change their practice, they need professional development opportunities that are in-depth and sustained.** In the words of one workshop participant, a one-shot workshop simplifies complex ideas until they become "meaningless mantras sold as snake oil." Many of the learning opportunities provided for teachers and other professionals violate the principles for optimizing learning. Teachers need opportunities to be involved in sustained learning, through teaching that models the methods that they are being urged to adopt. Again, time must be scheduled for teachers to engage in ongoing opportunities to learn. And arrangements with those who provide professional development opportunities must incorporate ongoing opportunities for contact between those who teach the professional development courses and their teacher-participants.

   • **The communities that interact with teachers on a regular basis, including parents and administrators, must be persuaded of the value of change.** When educational practices change, parents who had a very different type of education—particularly if that education was successful—will be skeptical. When parents are dissatisfied, they take their complaints to administrators. For the teacher to have the freedom to use research-based ideas in classrooms, those ideas need to be effectively and persuasively communicated to parents and administrators.

   • **Changing teaching practices will require an alignment with assessment practices.** Both parents and administrators tend to judge the value of new initiatives in terms of student achievement as measured by test scores. For parents and administrators to support research-based curricula, success in producing measurable achievement must be demonstrated.

RESPONSES FROM THE POLICY COMMUNITY

Those from the policy community who participated in the conference and workshop were a diverse group from the national, state, and school district levels of government. The ideas of this group were as diverse as their affiliations. If there was a common theme in this group at all, it was that a report like *How People Learn* will not have an impact on education policy unless its messages are communicated effectively for this audience. They made varied suggestions for next steps.

- **For research to be useful in policy arenas, it must emphasize the link between research findings and policies that address the practical issues of education.** Policy makers are concerned with the skills and competencies required for young people to succeed in (school or work) and to be active participants in their communities. Linking research findings to such goals will enhance their value to policy makers. The more closely research findings focus on the needs of the various communities served by the education system, the more useful those finding will be to the legislative process.

- **Presentations of education research must emphasize the scientific basis of the findings.** Deep skepticism is expressed by elected officials that there is much that is solid in the field of education research; many consider the field "soft" or "fluffy." The difference in levels of funding between the National Institutes of Health and the Office of Educational Research and Improvement reflects a judgment by policy makers regarding the scientific basis of the work these agencies undertake. If policy makers can be persuaded of the scientific basis of education research, the gap between spending on health research and on education research might be narrowed.

- **It would be useful to policy makers to highlight examples of education success stories that use research-based innovations.** Policy makers want to do the right thing for the education system, but they are uncertain as to what that right thing might be. Examples of successes that are research based and focused on student achievement are very valuable and influential in policy arenas.

- **Agreement between researchers and the education community on the needed changes must come first.** The messages of the report are primarily directed to the community of educators and teacher trainers. If these communities can agree among themselves and with education researchers on the changes that need to take place, then these agreements can be reflected in public policy. If such agreement is achieved, the high rate of teacher turnover expected in the years ahead will provide an opportunity for major change to be channeled through newly trained teachers.

- **The public must be educated and engaged.** For the findings from *How People Learn* to have an impact on education policy, the public needs to understand the significance of the findings, what they mean in the context of their own experiences and for their children, and how schools and school systems can realistically respond to the findings. If the public understands these issues, then they can influence their elected officials to think accordingly.

• **Researchers must communicate with policy makers more effectively.** To be useful to policy makers, research findings should be presented in a form that is brief, to the point, and jargon free. It must be targeted to specific policy audiences. School superintendents, state legislators, governors, and federal policy makers each have separate policy responsibilities. Each needs to have a brief description of key research findings as they relate to their area of concern. And since policy making tends to be reactive, learning opportunities need to be provided at opportune moments. They should not be limited to written materials, with which policy makers are inundated, but should include direct engagement in dialogue.

4

Proposing a
Research and Development Agenda

In designing a research and development agenda, the committee considered the mechanisms through which research influences practice, in light of the feedback received at the two events organized around *How People Learn*. Recall that Figure 1.1 from Chapter 1 depicts the committee's view of the paths through which research influences practice.

Several aspects of the figure are worth noting again here. First, the influence of research on the four mediating arenas—education materials, pre-service and in-service teacher and administrator education programs, public policy, and public opinion and the media—has typically been weak for the variety of reasons discussed earlier. Without clear communication of a research-based theory of learning and teaching, the operational theories held by the various stakeholders are not aligned. Teachers, administrators, and parents frequently encounter conflicting ideas about the nature of learning and its implications for effective teaching.

Second, with the exception of the relatively small set of cases in which teachers and researchers work together on design experiments, the arrows between research and practice in Figure 1.1 are one-way. This reflects the fact that practitioners typically have few opportunities to shape the research agenda and contribute to an emerging knowledge base of learning and teaching. The task of bridging research and practice requires an agenda that allows for a flow of information, ideas, and research questions in both directions. It requires an agenda that consolidates the knowledge base and strengthens the links between that knowledge base and each of the components that together influence practice.

The potential benefits of bridging theory and practice are noted by Donald Stokes in his recent work, *Pasteur's Quadrant* (1997). Stokes observed that many of the advances in science are intimately connected to the search for solutions to practical problems. Pasteur appears in the book's title because his work contributed so clearly to scientific understanding while simultaneously focusing on practical problems. Such research is "use-inspired." As in Pasteur's case, when executed as part of a systematic and strategic program of inquiry, it can support new understandings at the most fundamental and basic scientific level.

A central theme of Stokes's argument is that the typical linear conceptualization of research as a sequence from basic to applied is an inaccurate characterization of much research, and it is highly limiting for the envisioning of a research agenda. He proposes instead a quadrant in two-dimensional space in which considerations of use and the quest for fundamental understanding define the horizontal and vertical axes respectively. The quadrant allows for the possibility that research can be high in both basic and applied values.

The committee is sympathetic to this perspective. We envision the need for a comprehensive program of use-driven strategic research and development focused on issues of improving classroom learning and teaching. The facts that schools and classrooms are the focus and that enhanced practice and learning are the desired goals render the program of research no less important with respect to advancing the theoretical base for how people learn. Indeed, many of the advances described in *How People Learn* are the product of use-inspired research and development focused on solving problems of classroom practice.

It is worth noting that a wide array of quantitative and qualitative methods drawn from the behavioral and social sciences are employed in education research. The methods often vary with the nature of the learning and teaching problem studied and the level of detail at which issues are pursued. Given the complexity of educational issues in real-world contexts in which variables are often difficult to control, the types of "use-inspired" research that we envision will necessarily demand a variety of methods. These will range from controlled designs to case studies, with analytic methods for deriving conclusions and inferences including both quantitative and qualitative procedures of substantial rigor. To build an effective bridge between research and practice, such a multiplicity of methods is not only reasonable, it is essential. No single research method can suffice.

OVERARCHING THEMES

Adopting the perspective of use-inspired, strategic research and development focused on issues of learning and teaching is a powerful way to organize and justify the specific project areas we describe. In light of the many comments of workshop participants, the committee identified five overarching themes that guided our understanding of the change that is required to bridge research and practice more effectively. Three of these themes point to the consolidation of knowledge that would help link research and practice:

1. Elaborate the messages in *How People Learn* at a level of detail that makes them usable to educators and policy makers. Workshop participants were enthusiastic about the report and its implications for classroom teaching. They were virtually unanimous, however, in the view that the findings and their implications need to be substantially elaborated and incorporated into curricula, instructional tools, and assessment tools before their impact will be felt in the classroom. It is not enough to know, for example, that subject-matter information must be tied to related concepts if deep understanding and transfer of learning are the goals. Teachers must recognize which particular concepts are most relevant *for the subject matter that they teach.* And they need curriculum materials that support the effort to link information with concepts. Similarly, policy makers need to know quite specifically how the principles in *How People Learn* relate to state standards. In this sense, the *development* aspect of the agenda is critical.

2. Communicate the messages in *How People Learn* in the manner that is most effective for each of the audiences that influences educational practice. For teachers to teach differently and administrators and policy makers to support a different model of teaching, they need opportunities to learn about the recommended changes and to understand what they are designed to achieve. Research must be done on effective methods of communicating these ideas to teachers, administrators, and policy makers, each of whom have different information needs and different ways of learning. Similarly, teachers, administrators, and policy makers all emphasized that the public's beliefs regarding education influence how they do their jobs. They recommended research aimed at effectively communicating key ideas from *How People Learn* to the public

3. Use the principles in *How People Learn* as a lens through which to evaluate existing education practices and policies. *How People Learn* emphasizes that many existing school practices and policies are inconsistent with what is known about learning. But there are also havens of exemplary educational practice, and the report points to some of these as well. The education landscape is dotted with reform efforts and with institutes and centers that produce new ideas and new teaching materials. Educators, administrators, and policy makers are eager for help in sorting through what already exists. They want to know which of these current practices, training programs, and policies are in alignment with the principles in *How People Learn,* and which are in clear violation of them.

Moreover, educators emphasized that new ideas are introduced to schools one after another, and teachers become weary and skeptical that any new reform effort will be better than the last. Zealous efforts to promote the newest idea often overlook existing practices that are successful. An effort to identify such practices will build support from those who have long been engaged in teaching for understanding.

Together, these three themes suggest that an effective bridge between research and practice will require a consolidated knowledge base on learning and teaching that builds, or is cumulative, over time. Elaborating on the committee's conceptualization in Figure 1.1, this knowledge base appears at the center of Figure 4.1. Fed by research, it organizes, synthesizes, interprets, and communicates research findings in a manner that allows easy access and effective learning for those in each of the mediating arenas. Attending to the communication and information links between the knowledge base and each of the components of the model simultaneously enhances the prospect for the alignment of research ideas and practice.

Two additional themes that emerged from the discussions focus on *how* research should be conducted to strengthen its link to practice:

4. Conduct research in teams that combine the expertise of researchers and the wisdom of practitioners. Much of the work that is needed to bridge research and practice focuses on the education and professional development of teachers, the curriculum, instruction and assessment tools that support their teaching, and the policies that define the environment in which teaching takes place. These are areas about which practitioners have a great deal of knowledge and experience. Workshop participants emphasized the need to have educators partnered with researchers in undertaking these research projects. Such partnerships allow the perspectives and

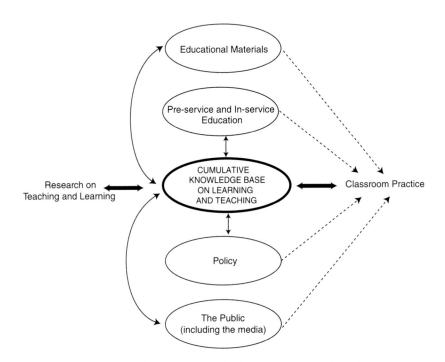

FIGURE 4.1 *Proposed model for strengthening the link between research and practice.*

knowledge of teachers to be tapped, bringing an awareness to the research of the needs and dynamics of a classroom environment. Since such partnerships are novel to many researchers, exemplary cases and guiding principles will need to be developed to make more likely the successful planning and conduct of research team partnerships.

5. Extend the frontier of learning research by expanding the study of classroom practice. Researchers and practitioners who participated in the workshops recommended expansion of research efforts that begin by observing the learning that takes place in the classroom. This research, as the earlier discussion of the Stokes work suggests, may advance understanding of the science of learning in important and useful ways.

Taken together, these latter two suggestions imply that the links between research and practice should routinely flow in both directions. The insights of researchers help shape the practitioner's understanding, and the insights of practitioners help shape the research agenda and the insights of researchers. Moreover, the link between each of the arenas and the knowledge base flows in both directions. Efforts to align teaching materials, teacher education, administration, public policy, and public opinion with the knowledge base are part of an ongoing, iterative research effort in which the implementation of new ideas, teaching techniques, or forms of communication are themselves the subject of study.

The agenda that follows proposes research and development that can help consolidate the knowledge base (which appears at the center of Figure 2.1) and can build the two-way links between the knowledge base and each of the arenas that influences practice. But that knowledge base is also fed by research on learning more generally and on classroom practice. The committee also suggests additional research that would strengthen the understanding of learning in areas that go beyond *How People Learn*.

Finally, since communication and access to knowledge are key to alignment, the committee proposes a new effort to use interactive technologies to facilitate communication of the variety of findings that would emerge from these research and development projects.

In many of the proposed areas for research and development, work is already under way. Inclusion in the agenda is not meant to overlook the contributions of research already done or in progress. Rather, we are inclusive in order to suggest that research findings need to be synthesized and integrated into the knowledge base and their implications tested through ongoing, iterative research.

RESEARCH AND DEVELOPMENT OF EDUCATIONAL MATERIALS

The goal of the recommended research and development in this area is to build on and elaborate findings in *How People Learn* so that they are "applications ready" and more usable to those responsible for developing curriculum, instructional, and assessment materials. It is designed to achieve three interrelated goals: (a) to identify existing educational materials that are aligned with the principles of learning suggested by the report and to develop and test new materials in areas of need, (b) to advance the knowledge base by significantly extending the work described in *How People Learn* to additional areas of curriculum, instructional techniques, and assessments that are in need of detailed analysis, and (c) to communicate the messages in *How People Learn* in a manner appropriate to developers of educational materials and teachers by using a variety of technologies (e.g., texts, electronic databases, interactive web sites). The research we recommend is described in this section in seven project areas.

Examining Existing Practice

1. Review a sample of current curricula, instructional techniques, and assessments for alignment with principles discussed in *How People Learn.* The committee recommends that teams of discipline-specific experts, researchers in pedagogy and cognitive science, and teachers review a sample of widely used curricula, as well as curricula that have a reputation for teaching for understanding. The envisioned research would involve two stages; these might be conducted together in a project, or as sequential projects.

Stage 1: These curricula and their companion instructional techniques and assessments should be evaluated with careful attention paid to alignment with the principles of learning outlined in *How People Learn.* The review might include consideration of the extent to which the curriculum emphasizes depth over breadth of coverage; the effectiveness of the opportunities provided to grasp key concepts related to the subject matter; the extent to which the curriculum provides opportunities to explore preconceptions about the subject matter; the adequacy of the factual knowledge base provided by the curriculum; the extent to which formative assessment procedures are built into the curriculum; and the extent to which accompanying summative assessment procedures measure understanding and ability to transfer rather than memory of fact.

The features that support learning should be highlighted and explained, as should the features that are in conflict. The report from this research should accomplish two goals. First, it should identify examples of curriculum components, instructional techniques, and assessment tools that incorporate the principles of learning. Second, the explication of features that support or conflict with the principles of learning should be provided in sufficient detail and in a format that allows the report to serve as a learning device for those in the education field who choose and use teaching and assessment tools. As such, it could serve as a reference document when new curricula and assessments are being considered.

Stage 2: The curricula that are considered promising should be evaluated to determine their effectiveness when used in practice. Curricula that are highly rated on paper may be very difficult for teachers to work with, or in the light of classroom practice may fail to achieve the level of under-standing for which they are designed. Measures of student achievement take center stage in this effort. Through the lens of *How People Learn,* achievement is indicated not only by a command of factual knowledge, but also by a student's conceptual understanding of subject matter and the ability to apply those concepts to future learning of new, related material. If exist-ing assessments do not measure conceptual understanding and knowledge transfer, then this stage will require development and testing of such measures. In addition to achievement scores, feedback from teachers and curriculum directors who use the materials would provide additional input for stage 2.

Ideally, the review of curricula would take place at several levels: at the level of curriculum units, which may span several weeks of instructional time; at the level of semester-long and year-long sequences of units; and at the level of multiple grades, so that students have chances to progressively deepen their understanding over a number of years.

The curricula reviewed should not be limited to those that are print based. As a subset of this effort, the committee recommends a review of curricula that are multimedia. The number of computers in schools is expand-ing rapidly. For schools to use that equipment to support learning, they must be able to identify the computer-based programs that can enhance classroom teaching or class assignments. The committee recommends that research be done to:

a. Identify technology programs or computer-based curricula that are aligned with the principles of learning for understanding. The programs identified should go beyond those that are add-ons of factual information or that simply provide information in an entertaining fashion. The investiga-tion should explore how the programs can be used as a tool to support knowledge-building in the unit being studied, and how they can further enhance the development of understanding of key concepts in the unit. The study should also explore the adequacy of opportunities for learning about the programs and for ongoing support in using the programs in a classroom setting;

b. Evaluate the aligned programs as teaching/learning tools by con-ducting empirical research on their distinctive contribution to achievement and other desired outcomes.

c. Investigate computer programs that appear to be effective teaching devices but do not clearly align with the principles of learning. These might suggest productive areas for further study.

Extend the Knowledge Base by Developing and Testing New Educational Materials

2. In areas in which curriculum development has been weak, design and evaluate new curricula, with companion assessment tools, that teach and measure deep understanding. As an extension of Recommendation 1 above, or in some cases as a substitute, the committee recommends the development and evaluation of new curriculum and assessment materials that reflect the principles of learning outlined in *How People Learn.* Once again, the committee recommends that the development be done by teams of disciplinary experts, cognitive scientists, curriculum developers, and expert teachers. Ideally, research in this category will begin with existing curricula and modify them to better reflect key principles of learning. In some cases, however, exemplary curricula for particular kinds of subject matter may not exist, so the teams will need to create them. This research and development might be coordinated with the ongoing efforts of the National Science Foundation to ensure complementary rather than duplicative efforts.

The curricula should be designed to support learning for understanding. They will presumably emphasize depth over breadth. The designs should engage students' initial understanding, promote construction of a foundation of factual knowledge in the context of a general conceptual framework, and encourage the development of metacognitive skills.

Companion teacher materials for a curriculum should include a "meta-guide" that explains its links to principles of learning, reflects pedagogical content knowledge concerning the curriculum, and promotes flexible use of the curriculum by teachers. The guide should include discussion of expected prior knowledge (including typical preconceptions), expected competencies required of students, and ways to carry out formative assessments as learning proceeds. Potentially excellent curricula can fail because teachers are not given adequate support to use them. Although instructional guides cannot replace teacher training efforts, the meta-guide should be both comprehensive and user-friendly to supplement those efforts. Finally, both formative and summative tests of learning and transfer should be proposed as well.

Once developed, the committee recommends field-testing of the curricula in order to amass data on student learning and teacher satisfaction, identifying areas for improvement. Clearly, it is easier to field-test short units rather than longer ones. Ideally, different research groups that are focusing on similar topics across different age groups (e.g., algebra in elementary, middle, and high school) would work to explore the degree to which each of the parts seems to merge into a coherent whole.

The committee recommends once again that careful attention be paid to the criteria used to evaluate the learning that is supported by the materials and accompanying pedagogy. Achievement should measure understanding of concepts and ability to transfer learning to new, related areas.

3. Conduct research on formative assessment. The committee recommends a separate research effort on formative assessment. The importance of making students' thinking visible by providing frequent opportunities for assessment, feedback, and revision, as well as teaching students to engage in self-assessment, is emphasized in *How People Learn* and in the proposals above. But the knowledge base on how to do this effectively is still weak. To bolster the understanding of formative assessment so that it can more effectively be built into curricula, this research effort should:

a. Formulate design principles for formative assessments that promote the development of coherent, well-organized knowledge. The goal of these assessments is to tap understanding rather than memory for procedures and facts;

b. Experiment with approaches to developing in students and teachers a view of formative assessment and self-assessment as an opportunity for providing useful information that allows for growth, rather than as an outcome measure of success or failure;

c. Explore the potential of new technologies that provide the opportunity to incorporate formative assessment into teaching in an efficient and user-friendly fashion.

This research effort should consider as well the relationship between formative and summative assessments. If the goal of learning is to achieve deep understanding, then formative assessment should identify problems and progress toward that goal, and summative assessment should measure the level of success at reaching that goal. Clearly they are different stages of the same process and should be closely tied in design and purpose.

4. Develop and evaluate videotaped model lessons for broadly taught, common curriculum units that appear throughout the K-12 education system. Many lessons and units of study are taught almost universally to students in the United States. Examples include the rain cycle in science, the concept of gravity in physics, the Civil War in history, and *Macbeth* in English. The committee recommends that a sample of familiar teaching topics be chosen to illustrate teaching methods that are compatible with the findings of *How People Learn*. The research and development should be undertaken by teams composed of disciplinary experts, pedagogical experts, master teachers, and video specialists. The model lessons or units envisioned by the committee would in all cases:

a. Illustrate a methodology for drawing out and working with student preconceptions and assessing progress toward understanding (results from project area 5 below could contribute to this endeavor);

b. Present the conceptual framework for understanding or organizing the new material;

c. Provide clear opportunities for transfer of knowledge to related areas. When appropriate, they would also:

d. Provide instruction on the use of meta-cognitive skills;

e. Include examples of group processes in the development of understanding, illustrating the nature (and potential advantages) of capitalizing on shared expertise in the classroom.

The model units would be prefaced and heavily annotated to guide the viewer's understanding. Annotations would include both subject content and pedagogical technique. Companion assessment tools should be developed that measure understanding of the core concepts taught in the lessons. The committee recommends multiple models of teaching the same unit in different school contexts. These could serve several purposes. First, the goal of the videotaped models is to illustrate effective approaches to teaching more generally, not just of teaching a particular unit. This learning is more likely to occur with multiple examples that allow for variation in the delivery of the lesson, holding constant the underlying principles of effective teaching.

Second, the classroom dynamics and level of preparation of the students can vary significantly from one school to the next. It may be difficult for a teacher to find relevant instruction in a videotape of a class that does not resemble the one in which she or he teaches. Finally, the art of teaching requires flexibility in responding to students' inquiries and reflections. Multiple cases can demonstrate flexibility in response to the particular students being taught while attending to a common body of knowledge.

Whether providing multiple models does indeed achieve these purposes is itself a research question worth pursuing. Such research should test the effect of each additional model provided on the level of understanding of key learning and teaching concepts, as well as the amount of variation between models that optimizes the flexibility of understanding that viewers achieve.

Once pilot versions of these lessons are designed, the committee recommends rigorous field-testing, with time built into the research plan for revision and retesting. Video-based materials already developed and in use as part of the National Board for Professional Teaching Standards training and assessment development process should be considered as possible candidate materials for further study as part of this process.

The committee recommends that the model lessons be organized in widely accessible video and multimedia libraries that could serve multiple purposes:

• The lessons could be used as anchors for discussions of pre-service and in-service teachers and administrators, as they try to understand and master the pedagogy to accompany the new forms of learning described in *How People Learn.*

• The lessons could be instructive in administrative training programs. School administrators responsible for hiring and evaluating teachers need models of good practice that can inform their evaluations.

• With some modified annotations, the lessons could inform parents about teaching techniques that promote learning for understanding. Changing classroom teaching can be problematic if new methods run counter to parents' perceptions of the learning process. The model lessons could help parents understand the goals of the espoused approach to teaching.

Extend the Knowledge Base Through Elaboration and Development of Key Research Findings

5. Conduct research on key conceptual frameworks, by discipline, for the units that are commonly taught in K-12 education. A key finding of the research reviewed in *How People Learn* is that deep understanding— and the transfer of learning that is one of its hallmarks—requires that the subject matter being taught be tied to the key concepts or organizing principles that the discipline uses to understand that subject. The goal of teaching about a given topic is not simply to convey factual information, although that information is a necessary component. The meaning of that information as it relates to basic concepts in the discipline, the related analytical methods that answer the question "How do we know," and the terms of discourse in a disciplinary field are all components in developing competence.

To illustrate, consider the topic of marine mammals as it might be taught in early elementary school. That unit would be likely to include identification of the various marine mammals, information on the features that distinguish marine mammals from fish, and perhaps more detailed information on the various types and sizes of whales, the relative size of male and female whales, etc. To the marine biologist, this information is the interesting detail in a larger story, which begins with the question: "Why are there mammals in the sea?" A unit organized around that question would engross students in an evolutionary tale in which the adaptation of sea creatures for life on the land takes a twist: land mammals now adapt to life in the sea. The core biological concepts of adaptation and natural selection would be at the center of the tale. Students would come to understand the puzzle that marine mammals posed for scientists: Could sea creatures evolve to mammals that live on land and then evolve again to mammals that return to the sea? They would come to understand the debate in the scientific community and the discovery of supporting evidence. And they would have cause to challenge the widespread misconception that evolution is a unidirectional process.

The approach of tying information on marine mammals to the concepts, language, and ways of knowing in that branch of science can be used in other areas of science, as well as in other disciplines. But the concepts and organizing principles that provide a framework for particular subject matter are often obvious only to those who are expert in the discipline. The committee recommends that discipline-specific research be conducted in history, mathematics, natural sciences, and social sciences to systematically review units of study that commonly appear in K-12 curricula, specifying the conceptual framework to which the unit should be tied. The results of this effort will allow teachers and curriculum developers to see if a common conceptual basis exists for separate units of study. Making those underlying concepts explicit helps students construct a model for understanding that facilitates transfer.

The committee further recommends that the work in each discipline be reviewed by a panel of disciplinary experts to identify consensus and contested areas. To the extent that there is a high level of agreement within a discipline about the organizing constructs as they apply to units of classroom study, the outcome of this research will be highly useful to those who design and evaluate curricula and to those who teach.

6. Identifying and addressing preconceptions by field. The research reviewed in *How People Learn* makes the case that new learning is built on the foundation of existing knowledge and preconceived notions regarding the subject of study. Learning is enhanced when preconceived understandings are drawn out. When these are accurate, new knowledge can be directly tied to what is already known. And when they are inaccurate, students can be made aware of how their existing conceptions fall short and be provided with more robust alternatives. Teachers and curriculum developers can build learning experiences into curricula that challenge typical misconceptions, and that draw out and work with unpredictable preconceptions. The committee recommends research by discipline and subject area:

a. To identify common preconceptions that students bring to the classroom at different levels of education;

b. To identify links that can be made between existing learner understandings and the disciplinary knowledge, when they are compatible;

c. To identify progressive learning sequences that would allow students to bridge naïve and mature understandings of the subject matter.

The research would be conducted independently for mathematics, natural sciences, social sciences, and humanities. The research teams should combine disciplinary experts with cognitive scientists, expert teachers, and curriculum developers. The range of topics covered in each disciplinary area should allow for exploration of the key concepts in the field as they arise in commonly covered course topics in the K-12 curriculum.

In some disciplines (e.g., physics), substantial research has already been done to identify misconceptions. This project should build on those efforts but extend them by developing and testing strategies for working with preconceptions, providing tools and techniques for teachers to work with in the classroom.

The research, as envisioned, would involve several stages:

• Stage 1 would involve the identification of the subject areas for study and the key concepts that students must comprehend in order to understand each subject area. Assessment tools that allow for a test of comprehension of these concepts, including tests of the degree to which students' understanding supports new learning (transfer), would also be developed at this stage.

• Stage 2 would consist of a review of existing research that explores the preconceptions that students bring to that subject area and an extension of the research into areas that have not been adequately explored.

• Stage 3 would involve the development of learning opportunities and instructional strategies that build on, or challenge, those preconceptions. These might include experiments in physics that produce results contradicting initial understandings, or research tasks in history that show the same event from multiple perspectives, challenging good-guy/bad-guy stereotyping.

- Stage 4 would involve experimental testing of the newly developed learning tools and instructional strategies, with the assessment tools developed in stage 1 used as a measure of comprehension.

The final products of this research in each disciplinary area would include written reports of research results, as well as descriptions of tested instructional techniques for working with student preconceptions. The findings could be incorporated into videotaped model lessons (project area 4 above) or those used in the pedagogical laboratories proposed in the project area 13.

Develop Tools for Effective Communication of the Principles of Learning as They Apply to Educational Materials

7. Develop an interactive communications site that provides information on curricula by field. Feedback from workshop participants suggested a high level of frustration with the task of sorting through and evaluating curricula. A central source of information on curricula and their major features would be highly valued. The committee recommends the development and maintenance of an interactive communications site that provides information about design principles for effective curricula, and relates these principles to particular curricula by subject area. The curriculum review and development recommended above would provide a solid foundation of information for creation of the site.

Comparing and rating curricula can be a difficult business. A good curriculum will need to balance coverage of information with in-depth exploration of concepts. But there is no magic balancing point. One curriculum may provide more opportunities to explore interesting scientific narratives, whereas another may offer more opportunities for valuable experimentation. But if the difficulty in evaluating curricula means backing away entirely from the effort to compare and evaluate, then the information available to those who must choose among curricula is diminished. Thousands of schools and teachers must then bear a much heavier burden of information collection.

The committee recommends a comprehensive evaluation process that does not rank-order curricula, but rather evaluates them on an array of relevant features. A sample of such features taken from *How People Learn* includes the extent to which the curriculum draws out preconceptions; whether it includes embedded assessment (both formative and summative); the extent to which it places information in the relevant conceptual framework; the extent to which curriculum modules can be reconfigured in ways that allow teachers to meet particular goals and needs, and the extent to which it encourages the development of metacognitive skills. Other useful information on the curriculum would include the extent and results of field-testing, the length of time it has been in use, the number of schools or school districts that have adopted it, the opportunities for teacher learning, and the amount and kind of support available to teachers using the curriculum. Information on student response to and interest in the curriculum would be useful as well.

Evaluating curricula in terms of their relevant features that align with the principles in *How People Learn* is a massive undertaking. For its ultimate success, such evaluations will need to represent expert judgments coming from different perspectives, including the subject-matter discipline, master teachers, learning and pedagogy experts, and curriculum developers. Users of an interactive communications site that publishes these judgments can then weigh the expertise they consider most useful for guiding their choice of curricula. The site should invite their feedback on experiences with using the curricula that this information led them to select. Ideally, the communications site will make it easy for teachers to access information that is directly relevant to their particular goals and needs.

Success will also require a growing group of constituencies and experts who can carry forward the principles in *How People Learn* to evaluating curricula.

RESEARCH ON PRE-SERVICE AND IN-SERVICE EDUCATION

The research and development proposed in this section is designed, once again, to achieve three goals: (a) to look first at existing practice through the lens of *How People Learn,* (b) to advance understanding in ways that would facilitate alignment of teacher preparation with principles of learning, and (c) to make the findings of this research more widely accessible and easily understood. The recommended research is described in seven project areas.

Examine Existing Practice Through the Lens of *How People Learn*

8. Review the structure and practices of teacher education for alignment with the principles of learning. For teacher education and professional development programs to be aligned with the principles of learning, they need to prepare teachers to think about the enterprise of teaching as building on the existing knowledge base and preconceptions of their students, to teach skills for drawing out and working with existing understandings, and to continually assess the progress of students toward the goal of deep understanding. The programs need to provide for their students the opportunity to develop a deep understanding themselves of the subject matter they will teach and the ability to facilitate students' transfer of knowledge to related areas. They need to prepare teachers to be aware of and directly teach metacognitive skills. And they need to convey a model of the teacher as learner, who continually develops expertise that is flexible and adaptive.

These are implications for *what* schools of education and professional development programs should teach. But the students in those programs will themselves learn more effectively if they are taught according to these principles. *How People Learn* therefore has implications for *how* schools of education do their job. Do those schools have program structures and practices that reflect the principles of learning discussed here?

The committee recommends that evaluation research be conducted to examine current program structures and practices at schools of education through the lens of *How People Learn*. This effort should not only synthesize what is already known about teacher training programs, but also undertake a new evaluation. The sample of schools should be chosen to reflect the wide range of program formats (which currently include undergraduate and postbaccalaureate program designs), as well as the widely varying enrollment demographics that exist across the more than 1,000 universities and colleges that offer teacher certification programs. The goal of this research is largely descriptive: to understand better how teachers are being trained relative to current understandings of learning, teaching, and the development of expertise; how much variation currently exists in teacher education programs; and the factors that contribute to such variability. Of special concern are program structures, course content, and instructional practices that seriously conflict with the principles of *How People Learn*. The proposed research should also bring into focus features of teacher education programs that correspond to the principles of learning, and that enhance the capability of future teachers to incorporate the principles into their practice.

9. Review professional development programs for alignment with the principles of learning and for relative effectiveness in changing teaching practice. The issue of teacher preparedness is rapidly becoming one of intense focus in policy arenas. Professional development programs are an important policy tool available to concerned lawmakers. But there are vastly different models of professional development, and relatively little is known about the amount and type that is required to significantly change teacher performance and student achievement. Existing research efforts along these lines need to be extended and built on.

The committee recommends that alternative models of professional development be reviewed for their alignment with the principles of learning. Features that promote or conflict with the principles should be highlighted. The research should also examine the effects of alternative types, and amounts, of professional development training on teacher performance and student achievement. As envisioned, the research would:

a. Define a small set of common models of professional development. These should include individual workshops, more lengthy in-service programs, and university courses. They should include training that is tied to a specific curriculum, as well as training in teaching techniques.

b. Review the features of those programs that do and do not support learning, including the opportunities they provide for exploring teachers' preconceptions, for assessing what teachers are learning as they go along, and for teachers to provide feedback and receive ongoing support as they attempt to use what they have learned in the classroom environment.

c. Define measures of teacher knowledge and performance that would be expected to change as a result of the learning opportunity.

d. Define measures of student achievement that would be expected to change as a result of the change in teaching.

e. Estimate the effect of quantity and type of training on teacher performance and student achievement.

The envisioned research would require a major data collection effort. Success is likely to require that researchers work closely with school districts over a multiyear period. In states or school districts that are about to undergo an expansion in professional development spending, conditions may be particularly ripe for such a partnership.

The results of this research should be written up separately for the three communities who are likely to find them useful: (a) for those who provide professional development programs, the results should provide feedback that allows for improvement in program design; (b) for administrators and policy makers, the results should provide guidance in evaluating professional development programs; and (c) for researchers, the results should be reported in detail sufficient to support further meta-analytic research.

10. Explore the efficacy of various types of professional development activities for school administrators. School administrators at the individual school and school district level are responsible for facilitating teacher learning and evaluating teacher performance. If they are to support teachers' efforts to incorporate the principles of learning into classroom practice, they will need professional development opportunities that provide an understanding of the principles and their enactment in a classroom environment.

The committee recommends that research be conducted to identify the amount and type of professional development needed to create in administrators an ability to differentiate between teaching practices that do, and do not, incorporate what is known about how people learn. This research should go beyond an effort to identify whether a particular professional development opportunity effectively changes administrators' evaluations of teacher performance. It should vary the amount of such training and the model through which training is provided (intensive workshops, monthly seminars conducted over the course of a year, etc.). Measures of administrators' interpretations of teaching should be taken prior to training, at the point of program completion, and again a year after completion in order to ascertain the sustainability of change over time and the effect of prior beliefs on post-training performance.

Extend the Knowledge Base Through Elaboration and Development of Key Research Findings

11. Conduct research on the preconceptions of teachers regarding the process of learning. Adults, as well as children, have preconceptions that contribute to the ways in which they make sense of ideas and evidence and the decisions they make in undertaking tasks. For teachers to think about and conduct their teaching differently, they need to learn, and the principles of learning should guide that effort. The committee therefore recommends that:

a. Research be conducted that explores the prior conceptions and beliefs of teachers and those learning to become teachers, identifying the common pedagogical models that current and prospective teachers use;

b. Learning opportunities be developed that challenge misconceptions about how people learn and support the development of a new model that is based on learning research;

c. Evaluations should be conducted of the effectiveness of those learning opportunities in changing understanding and conceptions of practice.

The outcome of this research would include both a description of common preconceptions about learning, as well as tested techniques for working with those preconceptions that could be incorporated into the curricula of schools of education and professional development programs.

12. Conduct discipline-specific research on the level and type of education required for teaching that discipline in elementary, middle, and high school. *How People Learn* makes clear that to teach effectively in any discipline, the teacher must link the information being taught to the key organizing principles of the discipline. To achieve this, the teacher must be provided with the discipline-specific training that allows for deep understanding of those principles. This type of teaching is not now a consistent feature of teacher training programs.

The committee recommends that discipline-specific research be conducted on the amount and type of training in content knowledge that teachers need for various levels of schooling (elementary, middle, high) in order to teach for understanding. The challenge in providing such training is to equip the future teacher with *both* content knowledge *and* an understanding of the thinking of children in the subject area at different developmental stages. Each is a critical component for effective teaching in a subject area. In light of this dual requirement, is content knowledge best obtained in disciplinary courses that also service majors in the discipline, or in courses in schools of education, or in jointly sponsored courses that emphasize effective teaching of the content of the discipline? When content and teaching methods are taught separately, are teachers able to bridge the two? When they are done together, is adequate attention given to the disciplinary content?

The committee recommends further that the discipline-specific research teams evaluate existing tools for assessing teachers' content knowledge and knowledge of discipline-specific developmental trajectories and make recommendations regarding their adequacy.

Develop Tools for Effective Communication of the Principles of Learning to Teacher Education

13. Develop model pedagogical laboratories. In many fields in which scientific principles must be put to work, laboratory experiences provide the opportunity to experiment with applications of general and specific principles. The expense of the laboratories is justified by the qualitatively different experience made possible when the boundaries of an idea can be tested or worked with in a laboratory or field-based setting.

To prepare students in schools of education to put to work the scientific principles of how people learn, laboratory experience could provide the opportunity to test the principles, become familiar with their boundaries, and learn how to make them operational. The committee therefore recommends the development of pilot pedagogical laboratories.

The teachers who worked with the committee emphasized that a first classroom experience can so overwhelm a teacher that what was learned in a preparatory program can quickly be cast aside. Norms of operating in a school can quickly be adopted as survival techniques, however divergent those norms and the principles of learning might be. Laboratory experience could provide the opportunities for practice, as well as for observation and diagnosis of events that are likely to arise in the classroom, that could ease the transition into the classroom and allow for greater transfer of school-based learning to the practice of teaching.

The laboratories, as envisioned, would have multiple purposes, the most important of which would be to provide teaching practice. The laboratories would need to develop ongoing relationships with a body of students to be taught (e.g., partnerships with local schools or Saturday classes). How this relationship would be established and maintained should be given careful attention in the design proposal for such a laboratory. Expert teachers who staff the laboratory would provide feedback and diagnosis of the teacher's lessons. The process could be aided by the use of a videotaped record of the instruction. The analysis could be further augmented by viewing tapes of other teachers who have attempted similar lessons. The teacher in training would work to improve the lesson through an iterative process of feedback and revision.

The laboratory setting would be ideal for helping teachers to develop the ability to conduct formative assessment techniques. A theme that has coursed through this report is that teachers must be able to draw out and work with students' preconceptions and assess their progress toward understanding. The laboratory could provide opportunities to develop those techniques under guided instruction.

The lab, as envisioned, would not provide a teaching internship or serve the function of a professional development school. Rather, it would provide an opportunity for beginning teachers to experiment with the principles of learning that are relevant to teaching practice. The goal is not to decontextualize teaching, but to create an environment in which the immediate demands of the classroom do not prevent reflection on, or exploration of, the process of learning. Exercises could be developed for laboratory use that involve cognitive science findings of relevance to teaching, including findings on memory, the organization of information, the use of metacognitive strategies, and retrieval of knowledge when transfer is prompted and when it is not. In addition to creating a deeper appreciation of the science of learning, these opportunities would invite teachers to think of themselves as scientists, to observe and reflect on learning as a scientist would. To the extent that those skills transfer to the classroom, the goal of continuous learning and reflection on practice will be well served.

The laboratories would also serve as a locus of information for teachers in training, for practicing teachers in the community, and for researchers in the learning sciences. "Protocol materials," or materials for diagnosis and interpretation, could be housed here. These might include model lessons or units (project area 4) that could be incorporated into the teaching of diagnostic and interpretive competencies. They might also include protocols of student creativity in scientific thinking, insight, reasoning like a novice versus an expert in a task, failure to transfer, negative transfer, distributed cognition, using parental stores of knowledge in a class, concrete and operational thinking, and inferring causation. These protocols, then, provide vivid cases and examples that instantiate concepts relevant to teaching and learning. Videotaped lessons of teaching in other countries produced by the Third International Mathematics and Science Study project might also be made available. Faculty-directed course projects could develop evaluations of curricula in terms of the principles of learning and submit them to the interactive communications site described above (project area 7) for broad use.

Technology centers could be housed in the laboratory as well. Computer programs to support classroom learning and technology-based curricula could be made available for exploration in this setting. Opportunities to connect with relevant communities of teachers and researchers via the Internet could also be explored. Students graduating from these programs will then carry to the schools in which they teach an ability to be connected to outside communities with relevant knowledge that is not now a feature in many school districts.

Well-equipped laboratories would be an asset in professional development activities as well as in pre-service training. As such, the laboratories could be used on a year-round basis.

14. Develop tools for in-service education that communicate the principles of learning in *How People Learn*. For the principles of learning to be incorporated into classroom practice, practicing teachers are a key audience. They are also a very busy audience. The challenge of developing ways to effectively communicate to those teachers is a central one. The committee recommends research and development that distills the messages of *How People Learn* for teachers and develops examples that are relevant to the classroom context. These messages should be communicated in a variety of formats, including text, audiotapes, videotapes, CD-ROMS, and Internet-based resources.

Researchers should design and study the effectiveness of the different media in communicating key ideas, as well as the satisfaction of teachers with the various media and the change in practice that ensues. This research should focus on the format of the material as well. For example, case-like stories could be compared with more didactic methods often used in texts and lectures.

RESEARCH ON EDUCATION POLICY

How People Learn, we have argued, suggests far-reaching reform of education. It has direct implications for what is taught in the classroom, how it is taught, the relationship between students and teachers, the content and role of assessments, and the preparation of those who undertake the daunting task of classroom teaching. Yet *How People Learn* is not a blueprint for redesigning schools.

Policy makers involved in the workshop were interested in the critical components of change that the report implies, as well as their associated costs. Given the task that is before them, this focus can be easily understood. But just as a doctor who recommends a healthy diet, stress reduction, exercise, adequate rest, and a personal support system cannot say which is most critical to health, researchers cannot identify the most critical change in the education system. The parts of the system cannot be isolated; the interactions among them have powerful influences on outcome.

And just as the exercise requirement has no single attached cost—it can be met by a run through the park or an indoor tennis game at a posh racket club—teaching for understanding has no obvious price tag attached. Eliciting and working with student ideas and preconceptions will be easier in a small class than in a larger one, just as exercise in a sports club will be easier in inclement weather. But with a diverse clientele, a doctor will do best to focus on the principle of raising the heart rate for a sustained period of time rather than dictate the method for achieving the goal. Similarly, we focus on the principles of teaching for understanding with the recognition that, in the diverse landscape of schooling, the manifestations of those principles will vary. This does not diminish what is known with certainty: teaching for understanding is a clear goal with several well-defined components (discussed in Chapter 2).

Our focus here is on policies that have a direct impact on attainment of those goals. Many of the research efforts already recommended will help inform policy; research on the efficacy of professional development programs, for example, will be of use to policy makers who set requirements for receiving funds for that purpose. At the urging of both policy makers and educators who participated in the workshop, we propose further research to review standards and assessments at the state level, and to examine teacher certification requirements at both the state and national level.

At the district level, reform can be notoriously difficult to implement or extend. In order to identify the policies that appear to facilitate or impede the adoption and expansion of new teaching practices, we propose case study research on schools and school districts that have successfully implemented reform. Although we don't envision a blueprint, there may be organizational features, operational policies, or incentive structures in these schools that create an environment conducive to change.

The recommended research is described in five project areas.

State Standards and Assessments

15. Review state education standards and the assessment tools used to measure compliance through the lens of *How People Learn.* Forty-nine states now have a set of education standards that apply to their schools, and most have or are developing assessment tools to hold school districts accountable for implementation. Standards vary considerably in the amount of control they exercise over what is taught, in the content they impose, and (implicitly or explicitly) in the model of learning that they imply. The committee recommends that a sample of state standards be reviewed through the lens of *How People Learn* for the following purposes:

a. To identify features of standards that support and violate the principles of learning in *How People Learn;*

b. To evaluate the alignment of desirable features in a state's standards with the assessment tools used for measuring compliance;

c. To evaluate the features of compliance assessments that support and conflict with the principles of learning;

d. To identify incentives and penalties that support the goal of effective education and those that appear to undermine that goal.

16. Conduct research on measures of student achievement that reflect the principles in *How People Learn* and that can be used by states for accountability purposes. Tests of student achievement that can be widely and uniformly administered across schools are the key mechanism by which policy makers hold schools accountable. *How People Learn* has clear implications for the measurement of student achievement. It suggests, for example, that recall of factual information is inadequate as a measure of deep understanding or as an indicator of the ability to transfer learning to new situations or problems.

Conventional psychological and educational testing is an outgrowth of theories of ability and intelligence that were current at the beginning of the century. Psychometrics has become increasingly sophisticated in its measurements; yet it does not attempt to look inside the "black box" of the mind. Now that the newer sciences of cognition and development have transformed our understanding of learning and the development of expertise, measurement theory and practice need fundamental rethinking. There is much in the traditional methods that is valuable, including a focus on objectivity and reliability of measurement. There is a problem, however, with what is being measured.

As a first step in the process of rethinking educational testing, the committee recommends that assessment tools be designed and tested with the goal of measuring deep understanding as well as the acquisition of factual knowledge. This is both a modest beginning and a challenging task. To be useful for policy purposes, these assessments should be in a form that can be administered widely and scored objectively and that meets reasonable standards of validity and reliability. These requirements can be at odds with the measurement of deep understanding, at least in the current state of the art. But it is important to begin finding solutions that, for example, minimize the trade-off between assessing for understanding and scoring objectively. A variety of experiments is needed, both with new forms of standardized tests (including computer-based instruments that permit "virtual" experiments), and with alternative assessments (such as portfolios) that have become more popular in recent years.

The committee further recommends research on assessment tools of different types to determine:

a. Whether alternative assessments yield significantly different measures of student achievement or highly correlated results.

b. How alternative assessment measures might be combined to offer a balanced view of achievement.

17. Review teacher certification and recertification requirements. Currently, 42 of the 50 states assess teachers as part of the certification and licensure process. But states vary enormously in the criteria used and the amount and type of assessment they require. The federal government also has provided support for an assessment process for advanced certification that is developed and administered by the National Board for Professional Teaching Standards. The committee recommends that research be conducted to review the requirements for teacher certification in a sample of states (selected for their diversity). Specific focus should be given to the types of assessments currently in use across the continuum of teacher development, from initial licensure to advanced status. This would include standardized tests, performance-based assessments under development (Interstate New Teacher Assessment and Support Consortium), and the National Board assessments. Efforts should be made to determine:

a. The features of certification that are aligned with the principles of *How People Learn* and those that are in conflict.

b. To the extent that data are available, the relationship between certification and increases in student learning.

This project should also recommend, when appropriate, strategies to reform certification processes so that they provide better signals of a teacher's preparedness for the task of teaching for understanding.

District-Level Policy

18. Conduct case study research of successful "scaling-up" of new curricula. School districts set a variety of policies that influence the environment in which teachers operate. Even when a new curriculum is pilot-tested with positive results, it can be very difficult to extend that curriculum into other schools in the district, sometimes even to other classrooms in the same school. The committee recommends case study research of successful scaling-up efforts to determine which district-level and school-level policies facilitated reform. The case studies should include information on features that teachers often identify as obstacles to reform:

a. How much scheduled time do teachers have in their work day that is not in the classroom and that can be used for reflection, study, or discussion with other teachers?

b. How much training was offered to teachers who adopted the new curriculum? Is there ongoing support for the teacher who has questions during implementation? Is there evaluation of the teacher's success at implementation?

c. Is there a community within the school, or extending beyond the school, that provides support, feedback, and an opportunity for discussion among teachers? Existing research suggests that the development of a professional community as part of the school culture is one of the most important determinants of successful school restructuring to implement a more demanding curriculum (Elmore, 1995; Elmore and Burney, 1996). These studies should focus on the features that hold that community together. Are there key players? Are there structured or informal opportunities for the exchange of ideas? What can be learned from these successes about the opportunities for enhancing teacher access to communities of learning using Internet tools?

d. Did the school attempt to involve parents and other community stakeholders in the change?

Some case study research of this type has already been done or is now under way. The effort to extend the knowledge base in this area should be coupled with an effort to synthesize the research results, making them easily accessible to school communities interested in reform.

Develop Tools for Effective Communication of the Principles in *How People Learn* to Policy Makers

19. Conduct research on the effective communication of research results to policy makers. Policy makers do not routinely look to research as a source of information and ideas. But there are windows of opportunity for research in policy making. Researchers who study this issue suggest that the windows are more likely to open during crises, when issues are new and policy makers have not yet taken a position, or when issues have been fought to a stalemate. When those opportunities arise, information must be communicated to policy makers in a manner that optimizes the chance that they will learn from research findings.

The committee recommends that research be conducted to:

a. Assess preconceptions of education policy makers regarding the goals of K-12 education and the strategies for achieving those goals. Are they consistent with the principles of learning in *How People Learn?*

b. Identify examples that engage the preconceptions of policy makers (if those preconceptions diverge from research findings on how people learn) and test their effectiveness at changing the initial understanding.

c. Identify methods of communication that are most likely to reach, and teach, policy makers.

d. Compare the effectiveness of alternative approaches, including concisely written materials, personal contact, and briefings or seminars.

The product of this research should be both a report of the findings regarding how policy makers learn most effectively and concisely written material that can be used for communicating effectively to policy makers.

PUBLIC OPINION AND THE MEDIA

Information communicated to the public through the media can influence practice in two ways. First, to the extent that the public is aware of the implications of learning research for classroom practice, teachers, administrators, and policy makers will receive more support for the types of changes that *How People Learn* suggests. Second, many teachers, administrators, and policy makers themselves are influenced by ideas that reach them through popular media. As we heard from participants in the workshops, *How People Learn* is not a document that is likely to be widely read by educators and policy makers. Information presented in a more popular format will have far better prospects of reaching this audience.

20. Write a popular version of *How People Learn* for parents and the public. Everyone has preconceptions regarding the process of learning and effective methods of education. Those theories are put to work on a daily basis when we model behaviors for children, provide instructions to coworkers, or explain a problem to a friend. These models are likely to be influenced by personal experience.

The translations of these experience-based models to the evaluation of classroom teaching can lead to expectations that conflict with the principles of learning drawn from research. A parent who is accustomed to teaching a child through direct instruction, for example, may be baffled by mathematics homework that requires the child to find a method of adding five two-digit numbers, rather than instructing the child to line those numbers in columns and add the columns in turn. The importance of grappling with the problem and searching for a solution method, and the appreciation that such grappling brings to the conventional method of solution, can be lost on the parent.

How People Learn develops many concepts and ideas that could inform parents about models of learning that are research based, thus influencing the criteria that parents use to judge classroom practice. But those ideas are embedded in a report that is not designed specifically to communicate to parents. The committee recommends the writing of a popular version of *How People Learn.* The popular presentation should address common preconceptions held by the public regarding learning. It should couch research findings in multiple examples that are relevant to parents' observations of children at a variety of ages. And it should help parents who are interested in understanding or evaluating a school formulate questions and make observations.

Some particularly effective examples and their implications for teaching should be highlighted in a manner that makes them easy to extract from the text. The children's book, *Fish is Fish* by Leo Lionni (1970) mentioned in *How People Learn,* can serve as an effective example. In the story, a frog adventures onto the land and comes back to describe what it saw. The fish who listen to the frog imagine each description to be an adaptation of a fish: humans are imagined to have fish bodies but walk upright, etc. The visual image powerfully describes the problem of presenting new information without regard to the learner's existing conceptions. Examples such as these would allow the popular media to communicate key ideas to the broader public who might not read the report.

The popular version of the report should itself be a subject of study. The committee proposes that a second stage of this project should involve research to assess whether the popular report effectively communicates its messages to a sample of parents.

BEYOND *HOW PEOPLE LEARN*

The research and development agenda proposed thus far focuses on the question that the Office of Educational Research and Improvement posed to the committee: How can the insights from *How People Learn* be incorporated into educational practice? *How People Learn* reviews a burgeoning literature that, taken collectively, provides the foundation for a science of learning. But more work needs to be done to extend that foundation. The committee proposes three research projects that hold promise for advancing the understanding of learning in ways that will be useful for educational practice.

21. Investigate successful and creative educational practice. There are well-known cases of exceptional teaching by educators who, often without the help of educational researchers, have created innovative and successful classrooms, programs, curricula, and teaching techniques. The committee recommends that case study research be conducted to investigate the principles of learning that underlie successful educational experiments. The conceptual framework provided by *How People Learn* can be employed as a lens through which that practice can be viewed, and such case studies could challenge and inform the science of learning.

The research would have several potential benefits: it would ground in sound theory innovations that often exist in isolation, that often cannot be evaluated well by traditional methods, and that cannot be explained well to others. This research could contribute an understanding of why the innovations work, perhaps leading to improvements in them. Moreover, it may stimulate researchers to pursue new theoretical questions regarding cognition. In innovative classrooms, students may engage in forms and levels of learning that are not anticipated by current cognitive theory. From studying such classrooms and the learning that takes place in them, researchers may modify their conceptions about learning.

22. Investigate the potential benefits of collaborative learning in the classroom and the design challenges that it imposes. Outside the classroom, much learning and problem solving takes place as individuals engage with each other, inquire of those with skills and expertise, and use resources and tools that are available in the surrounding environment. The benefits of this "distributed cognition" are tapped inside the classroom when students work collaboratively on problems or projects, learning from each others' insights, and clarifying their own thinking through articulation and argument (Vye et al., 1998a). Some research indicates that group problem solving is superior to individual problem solving (e.g., Evans, 1989; Newstead and Evans, 1995), and that developmental changes in cognition can be generated from peer argumentation (Goldman, 1994; Habermas, 1990; Kuhn, 1991; Moshman, 1995a, 1995b; Salmon and Zeitz, 1995; Youniss and Damon, 1992), and peer interaction (Dimant and Bearison, 1991, Kobayashi, 1994). For these reasons, the community-centered classroom described in Chapter 2, in which students learn from each other, can have substantial benefits.

But working in groups can have drawbacks for learning as well, particularly in the early grades. Societal stereotypes or classroom reputations can determine who takes the lead, and whose ideas are respected or dismissed. Differences in temperament can produce consistent leaders and followers. Group products can advance each members' understanding of a problem, or they can mask a lack of understanding by some.

The committee recommends that research be conducted by teams of cognitive scientists, developmental psychologists, curriculum developers, and teachers to investigate the potential benefits of collaborative learning in the classroom and the problems that must be addressed to make it beneficial for all students. The research should explore and field-test alternative design strategies. The results should be presented both as scholarly research, and as a discussion addressed to teachers who are interested in collaborative learning in the classroom.

23. Investigate the interaction between cognitive competence and motivational factors. Much of the research on learning has been conducted outside the classroom. Inside the classroom, issues of cognitive competence are intertwined with issues of motivation to perform. The challenges of learning for today's world require disciplined study and problem solving from the earliest grades. To meet the challenges, learners must be motivated to pay attention, complete assignments, and engage in thinking.

Although cognitive psychologists have long posited a relationship between learning and motivation, they have paid little attention to the latter, despite its vital interest to teachers. Research has been done on motivation, but there is no commonly accepted unifying theory, nor a systematic application of what is known to educational practice (National Research Council, 1999b).

The committee recommends that research be conducted to elucidate how student interests, identities, self-knowledge, self-regulation, and emotion interact with cognitive competence. This research should combine the efforts of social and developmental psychologists with those of cognitive psychologists. A variety of approaches should be considered, including case studies of small numbers of individual children and the study of the classroom practice of teachers with reputations for promoting achievement among average students, as well as those at high risk for failure.

24. Investigate the relationship between the organization and representation of knowledge and the purpose of learning that knowledge. Research in cognitive science suggests that knowledge is organized differently depending on the uses that need to be made of it. In other words, the structure of knowledge and memory and the conditions under which it is retrieved for application evolves to fit the uses to which it is put. Similarly, what counts as understanding will also be defined in terms of means, rather than as an end in itself. Just as there is no perfect map, but only maps that are useful for particular kinds of tasks and answering particular kinds of questions, there is no perfect state of understanding, but only knowledge organizations that are more or less useful for particular kinds of tasks and questions.

For example, relatively superficial knowledge of the concept of gold may be sufficient to differentiate a gold-colored watch from a silver-colored watch. But it would not be sufficient to differentiate a genuine gold watch from one made of other gold-colored metals or alloys, or fool's gold from the real thing.

This empirical insight has profound implications for the organization of education, teacher education, and curriculum development. The committee recommends research to deepen understanding of the kinds of knowledge organizations that will best support particular kinds of activities. For example, the kinds of biology needed to know how to take care of plants (e.g., knowing when, where, and how to plant them in different climates and soil conditions) differs from the knowledge necessary to genetically engineer them.

These kinds of issues become particularly important when considering the nature of the content knowledge that teachers need in order to teach various disciplines. For example, the most useful knowledge for a middle school mathematics teacher may not come from taking a higher-level course in a traditional mathematics sequence, particularly if that course was designed for the uses of that knowledge by mathematics and engineering students in problems suited to the work activities of those disciplines. Instead, it may come from a course that integrates mathematics with particular kinds of inquiry involving design and other tasks.

These considerations are also important for curriculum. Research investigations could yield better understanding for guiding curriculum design so that the knowledge that learners develop from their experiences in courses will be better retrieved in anticipated contexts of use for that knowledge. For example, too little is known about the kinds of activities in which an educated person—but not a future scientist—will be expected to use the scientific knowledge that they may acquire in science courses. Research on these considerations is important to pursue.

COMMUNICATING RESEARCH KNOWLEDGE

When one considers the complexity of the ways in which research influences practice (as depicted in Figure 1.1), the heterogeneous audiences for research and their very different needs become apparent. As we have noted throughout this report, the ways in which the principles of learning depicted in *How People Learn* will be incorporated into practice raise unique problems for pre-service and in-service education, for educational materials, for policy, and for the public (including the media). The pathways by which research knowledge travels, and the transformations it must undertake for each of these audiences, raise striking challenges for communications design. To be effective, such communications cannot serve merely as disseminations of research knowledge. Translating and elaborating that knowledge for each audience has been a theme throughout the agenda. In this final section, we propose an effort to make these translations widely accessible.

25. Design and evaluate ways to easily access the cumulative knowledge base. Adaptive communications about the science of learning are very much needed that can evolve to fit the distinctive needs of the various education audiences for knowledge derived from research. For such conversations to occur between the research communities and these diverse constituencies, experimentation with Internet-based communications forums is needed.

The Internet is becoming a social place for the formation and ongoing activities of distributed communities, not only a digital library for browsing and downloading information. Current electronic communities with tens of thousands of members share information and convene around a broad range of topics. High-quality resources on the science of learning will be needed to spur on-line discussions among the communities they are designed to serve, and to invite suggestions about how communications concerning the science of learning can better fit the needs of those who will use their results (Pea, 1999). Today one may find a great range of web sites that are devoted to education. But far fewer are devoted to research advances, much less their alignment with educational materials, practices, or policies that are depicted in the web sites.

The committee recommends the development and continuous improvement of a national communications forum for research knowledge on learning and teaching. This new media communications forum would be accessible through the Internet and would provide illustrative cases and usable information about both the research depicted in *How People Learn* and new findings that will continue to emerge in ongoing research. It would provide opportunities for different contributors who are stakeholders in education to post messages and rate the usefulness of documents and materials. Experimentation is needed in establishing "virtual places" online where diverse groups could convene to reflect on how these research advances could be incorporated to improve the practices of education and learning. Such a "learning improvement portal" would provide a vital national resource, guiding research-informed improvements of education.

CONCLUSION

The research efforts that we have proposed make a serious effort to combine the strengths of the research community with the insights gained from the wisdom and challenges of classroom practice. Our suggestions for research do not assume that basic research should first be conducted in isolation and then handed down to practitioners. Instead, we propose that researchers and practitioners work together to identify important problems of inquiry and define the kinds of research and communication strategies that would be most helpful to both groups.

Because of our emphasis on bridging research and practice, many of the efforts that we have proposed here are nontraditional. They combine research and development, rather than undertaking the two separately. It is the committee's view that such combined efforts are most likely to focus the attention of researchers on problems that are central to education, and they are more likely to ensure rigor and consistency with the principles of learning in the programs and products that are developed.

Moreover, many of the efforts combine research and communication. Often, the two are considered separate domains. But the goal of communication is learning, and *How People Learn* provides guidance for effective communication. For each audience, preconceived understandings must be identified and addressed in the effort to communicate. And examples that situate ideas in experiences relevant for that audience are crucial.

Combining expertise for the proposed projects will be challenging. There are still relatively few arenas in which researchers work as partners with teachers, administrators, and communications developers (who might film model lessons, develop web sites, produce brochures, etc.). But to be effective, systematic efforts to reform education will require that more of these partnerships be forged. Research and development grants that reward existing partnerships and encourage new ones to be formed could provide a much-needed impetus.

And finally, the agenda proposed is expansive. Many of the recommended projects are time-intensive, multiyear efforts. The nation's decentralized education system is vast. To don the lens of *How People Learn* to evaluate the various facets of that system is in itself a daunting task. We propose further the development and testing of new classroom teaching tools, techniques of teacher and administrator training, further research on human learning, and applications of technology that could provide dynamic mechanisms for bringing advances in how people learn and how people teach into continual cycles of coordination and improvement. From the committee's perspective, the integration of these efforts holds the potential to bring research and practice together in the interest of improved education.

References

Brice-Heath, S.
  1981   Toward an ethnohistory of writing in American. Pp. 25-45 in *Writing: The Nature, Development, and Teaching of Written Communication* (Vol. 1), M.F. Whiteman, ed. Hillsdale, NJ: Erlbaum.
  1983   *Ways with Words: Language, Life and Work in Communities and Classrooms.* Cambridge, England: Cambridge University Press.

Brown, A.L., and J.C. Campione
  1994   Guided discovery in a community of learners. Pp. 229-270 in *Classroom Lessons: Integrating Cognitive Theory and Classroom Practices*, K. McGilly, ed. Cambridge, MA: MIT Press.

Carey, S., and R. Gelman
  1991   *The Epigenesis of Mind: Essays on Biology and Cognition.* Hillsdale, NJ: Erlbaum.

Clement, J.
  1982   Student preconceptions of introductory mechanics. *American Journal of Physics* 50:66-71.

Diamat, R.J., and D.J. Bearison
  1991   Development of formal reasoning during successive peer interactions. *Developmental Psychology* 27:277-284.

DiSessa, A.
  1982   Unlearning Aristotelian physics: A study of knowledge-base learning. *Cognitive Science* 6:37-75.

Duckworth, E.
  1987   *"The Having of Wonderful Ideas" and Other Essays on Teaching and Learning.* New York: Teachers College Press, Columbia University.

Dweck, C.S.
  1989   Motivation. Pp. 87-136 in *Foundation for a Psychology of Education*, A. Lesgold and R. Glaser, eds. Hillsdale, NJ: Erlbaum.
Dweck, C., and E. Legget
  1988   A social-cognitive approach to motivation and personality. *Psychological Review* 95:256-273.
Elmore, R.F.
  1995   Getting to Scale with Successful Education Practices: Four Principles and Some Recommended Actions. Paper commissioned by the Office of Reform Assistance and Dissemination, U.S. Department of Education.
Elmore, R.F., Consortium for Policy Research in Education, and D. Burney
  1996   Staff Development and Instructional Improvement Community District 2, New York City. Paper prepared for the National Commission on Teaching and America's Future.
Evans, J. St. B. T.
  1989   *Bias in Human Reasoning*. Hillsdale, NJ: Erlbaum.
Fleming, D.S.
  1988   *The Literature on Teaching Utilization of Research: Implications for the School Reform Movement*. Andover, MA: The Regional Laboratory for Educational Improvement of the Northeast and Islands.
Gardner, H.
  1991   *The Unschooled Mind: How Children Think and How Schools Should Teach*. New York: Basic Books.
Gelman, R., and C.R. Gallistel
  1978   *The Children's Understanding of Number*. Cambridge, MA: Harvard University Press.
Goldman, A.I.
  1994   Argument and social epistemology. *Journal of Philosophy* 91:27-49.
Greeno, J.
  1991   Number sense as situated knowing in a conceptual domain. *Journal for Research in Mathematics Education* 22(3):170-218.
Habermas, J.
  1990   *Moral Consciousness and Communicative Action*. Cambridge, MA: MIT Press.
Harvard-Smithsonian Center for Astrophysics, Science Education Department
  1987   *A Private Universe*. Video. Cambridge, MA: Science Media Group.
Hatano, G.
  1990   The nature of everyday science: A brief introduction. *British Journal of Developmental Psychology* 8:245-250.
Hendrickson, G., and W.H. Schroeder
  1941   Transfer of training in learning to hit a submerged target. *Journal of Education Psychology* 32:205-213.

Holyoak, K.J.
  1984   Analogical thinking and human intelligence. Pp. 199-230 in *Advances in the Psychology of Human Intelligence* (Vol. 2), R.J. Sternberg, ed. Hillsdale, NJ: Erlbaum.

Hutchins, E.
  1995   *Cognition in the Wild.* Cambridge, MA: MIT Press.

Judd, C.H.
  1908   The relation of special training to general intelligence. *Education Review* 36:28-42.

Kobayashi, Y.
  1994   Conceptual acquisition and change through social interaction. *Human Development* 37:233-241.

Kuhn, D.
  1991   *The Skills of Argument.* Cambridge, England: Cambridge University Press.

Lave, J., and E. Wegner
  1991   *Situated Learning: Legitimate Peripheral Participation.* New York: Cambridge University Press.

Lin, X.D., and J. Lehman
  1999   Supporting learning of variable control in a computer-based biology environment: Effects of prompting college students to reflect on their own thinking. *Journal of Research in Science Teaching.* In press.

Lionni, L.
  1970   *Fish Is Fish.* New York: Scholastic Press.

Minstrell, J.
  1989   Teaching science for understanding. Pp. 130-131 in *Toward the Thinking Curriculum: Current Cognitive Research,* L.B. Resnick and L.E. Klopfer, eds. Alexandria, VA: Association for Supervision and Curriculum Development.

Moll, L.C.
  1986a   Creating Strategic Learning Environments for Students: A Community-Based Approach. Paper presented at the S.I.G. Language Developed Invited Symposium Literacy and Schooling, Annual Meeting of the American Educational Research Association, San Francisco, California.
  1986b   Writing as a communication: Creating strategic learning environments for students. *Theory into Practice* 25:102-108.
  1990   *Vygotsky and Education.* New York: Cambridge University Press.

Moll, L.C., J. Tapia, and K.F. Whitmore
  1993   Living knowledge: The social distribution of cultural sources for thinking. Pp. 139-163 in *Distributed Cognitions,* G. Salomon, ed. Cambridge, UK: Cambridge University Press

Moshman, D.
  1995a   Reasoning as self-constrained thinking. *Human Development* 38:53-64.
  1995b   The construction of moral rationality. *Human Development* 38:265-281.

National Research Council
   1999a   *How People Learn: Brain, Mind, Experience, and School.* Committee on Developments in the Science of Learning. Washington, DC: National Academy Press.
   1999b   *Improving Student Learning: A Strategic Plan for Education Research and Its Utilization.* Committee on Feasibility Study for a Strategic Education Research Program. Washington, DC: National Academy Press.
Newstead, S.E., and J. St. B.T. Evans, eds.
   1995   *Perspectives on Thinking and Reasoning: Essays in Honour of Peter Wason.* Hillsdale, NJ: Erlbaum.
Novick, L.R., and K.J. Holyoak
   1991   Mathematical problem solving by analogy. *Journal of Experimental Psychology: Learning, Memory, and Cognition* 17(3)(May):398-415.
Palincsar, A.S., and A.L. Brown
   1982   Reciprocal teaching of comprehension monitoring activities. *Cognition and Instruction* 1:117-175.
Pea, R.D.
   1999   New media communication forums for improving education research and practice. In *Issues in Education Research: Problems and Possibilities*, E.C. Lagemann and L.S. Shulman, eds. San Francisco: Jossey Bass.
Prawaf, R.S., J. Remillard, R.T. Putnam, and R.M. Heaton
   1992   Teaching mathematics for understanding: Case study of four fifth-grade teachers. *Elementary School Journal* 93:145-152.
Salmon, M.H., and C.M. Zeitz
   1995   Analyzing conversational reasoning. *Informal Logic* 17:1-23.
Scardamalia, M., C. Bereiter, and R. Steinbach
   1984   Teachability of reflective processes in written composition. *Cognitive Science* 8:173-190.
Schoenfeld, A.H.
   1983   Problem solving in the mathematics curriculum: A report, recommendation and annotated bibliography. *Mathematical Association of America Notes* No. 1.
   1984   *Mathematical Problem Solving.* Orlando, FL: Academic Press.
   1991   On mathematics as sense making: An informal attack on the unfortunate divorce of formal and informal mathematics. Pp. 331-343 in *Informal Reasoning and Education*, J.F. Voss, D.N. Perkins, and J.W. Segal, eds. Hillsdale, NJ: Erlbaum.
Stokes, D.E.
   1997   *Pasteur's Quadrant: Basic Science and Technological Innovation.* Washington, DC: Brookings Institution Press.
Suina, J.H., and L.B. Smolkin
   1994   From natal culture to school culture to dominant society culture: Supporting transitions for Pueblo Indian students. Pp. 115-130 in *Cross-cultural*

Roots of Minority Child Development, P.M. Greenfield and R.R. Cocking, eds. Hillsdale, NJ: Erlbaum.

Vosniadou, S., and W.F. Brewer
   1989   The Concept of the Earth's Shape: A Study of Conceptual Change in Childhood. Unpublished paper. Center for the Study of Reading, University of Illinois, Champaign.

Vye, N.J.., S.R. Goldman, C. Hmelo, J.F. Voss, S. Williams, and Cognition and Technology Group at Vanderbilt
   1998   Complex mathematical problem solving by individuals and dyads. *Cognition and Instruction* 15(4).

Vye, N.J., D.L. Schwartz, J.D. Bransford, B.J. Barron, L. Zech, and Cognition and Technology Group at Vanderbilt
   1998   SMART environments that support monitoring, reflection, and revision. In *Metacognition in Educational Theory and Practice*, D. Hacker, J. Dunlosky, and A. Graessner, eds. Mahwah, NJ: Erlbaum.

Wellman, H.M.
   1990   *The Child's Theory of Mind.* Cambridge, MA: MIT Press.

White, B.Y., and J.R. Fredrickson
   1997   *The ThinkerTools Inquiry Project: Making Scientific Inquiry Accessible to Students.* Princeton, New Jersey: Center for Performance Assessment, Educational Testing Service.
   1998   Inquiry, modeling, and metacognition: Making science accessible to all students. *Cognition and Science* 16:90-91.

Youniss, J., and W. Damon.
   1992   Social construction in Piaget's theory. Pp. 267-286 in *Piaget's Theory: Prospects and Possibilities*, H. Berlin and P.B. Pufal, eds. Hillsdale, NJ: Erlbaum.

A

Meeting Participants

CONFERENCE ON LEARNING RESEARCH AND EDUCATIONAL PRACTICE

Friday, December 18, 1998

Bruce Alberts, National Research Council
Robert Bain, University of Michigan, Ann Arbor
David Berliner, Arizona State University, Tempe
John Bransford, Vanderbilt University
Deanna Burney, Camden City Schools, Camden, NJ
Myrna Cooney, Taft Middle School, Cedar Rapids, IA
Ron Cowell, Education Policy and Leadership Center, Harrisburg, PA
Arthur Eisenkraft, Bedford Public Schools, Bedford, NY
Karen Fuson, Northwestern University
Herbert Ginsburg, Teachers College, Columbia University
Robert Glaser, Learning Research and Development Center, University of
    Pittsburgh
Louis Gomez, Northwestern University
Paul Goren, John D. and Catherine T. MacArthur Foundation
William Greenough, University of Illinois
Janice Jackson, Boston College
Jack Jennings, Center on Education Policy, Washington, DC
Jean Krusi, Ames Middle School, Ames, IA
Gloria Ladson-Billings, University of Wisconsin

Lucy Mahon, District 2, New York, NY

Kerry Mazzoni, California State Assembly

C. Kent McGuire, U.S. Department of Education, Office of Educational Research and Improvement

José Mestre, University of Massachussetts

Robert Morse, St. Alban's School, Washington, DC

Linda Nathan, Boston Arts Academy

Annemarie Palincsar, University of Michigan, Ann Arbor

Roy Pea, SRI International, Menlo Park, CA

James Pellegrino, Vanderbilt University

Penelope Peterson, Northwestern University

Thomas Romberg, University of Wisconsin

Carol Stewart, Office of the Governor, Columbia, SC

WORKSHOP ON LEARNING RESEARCH AND EDUCATIONAL PRACTICE

January 13-14, 1999

Amy Alvarado, Sanders Corner Elementary School, Ashburn, VA

Karen Bachofer, San Diego City Schools, San Diego, CA

Robert Bain, University of Michigan, Ann Arbor

David Berliner, Arizona State University, Tempe

John Bransford, Vanderbilt University

Cathy Cerveny, Logan Elementary School, Baltimore, MD

Rodney Cocking, National Research Council

Cathy Colglazier, McLean High School, Fairfax, VA

Myrna Cooney, Taft Middle School, Cedar Rapids, IA

Ron Cowell, Education Policy and Leadership Center, Harrisburg, PA

Suzanne Donovan, National Research Council

Arthur Eisenkraft, Bedford Public Schools, Bedford, NY

Jean Krusi, Ames Middle School, Ames, IA

Luna Levinson, U.S. Department of Education

José Mestre, University of Massachusetts

Robert Morse, St. Alban's School, Washington, DC

Barbara Scott Nelson, Center for the Development of Teaching, Education Development Center, Newton, MA

Annemarie Palincsar, University of Michigan, Ann Arbor

Ron Pedone, U.S. Department of Education

James Pellegrino, Vanderbilt University
Iris Rotberg, George Washington University
Leona Schauble, University of Wisconsin
Carol Stewart, South Carolina Chamber of Commerce, Columbia, SC
Lucy West, PS/IS 89, Math Initiative, New York, NY
Alexandra Wigdor, National Research Council

B

Biographical Sketches

JOHN D. BRANSFORD (Co-chair) is Centennial professor of psychology and co-director of the Learning Technology Center at George Peabody College of Education and Human Development, Vanderbilt University. He is also a senior research scientist at the university's John F. Kennedy Center and senior fellow at the Institute of Public Policy Studies. His research has focused primarily on the nature of thinking and learning and their facilitation, with special emphasis on the importance of using technology to enhance learning. His projects include the videodisc-based Jasper Woodbury Jasper Problem Solving Series, the Little Planet Literacy Series, and other projects that involve uses of technology to enhance thinking and learning in literature, science, history, and other areas. Bransford currently serves as a co-chair for the National Research Council's Committee on Developments in the Science of Learning and is a member of the National Academy of Education. He has a Ph.D. in cognitive psychology from the University of Minnesota.

JAMES W. PELLEGRINO (Co-chair) is the Frank W. Mayborn professor of cognitive studies at the Peabody College of Education and Human Development at Vanderbilt University. His research focuses on the application of cognitive research and technology to instructional problems on human cognition and cognitive development. Dr. Pellegrino currently serves on the National Research Council's Committee on Foundations of Educational and Psychological Assessment. He has been a faculty member at the University of Pittsburgh and at the University of California, Santa Barbara. He has a B.A. in psychology from Colgate University and M.A. and Ph.D. degrees from the University of Colorado, both in experimental, quantitative psychology.

DAVID BERLINER is professor of educational leadership and policy studies, professor of curriculum and instruction, and professor of psychology in education at Arizona State University. His recent research has focused on the study of teaching, teacher education, and education policy. His publications include *Putting Research to Work in Your Schools* (1993, with U. Casanova) and *A Future for Teacher Education* (1996). Dr. Berliner currently serves on the National Research Council's Board on Testing and Assessment. Among his many awards are the research into practice award of the American Educational Research Association, and the Distinguished Service Award of the National Association of Secondary School Principals. He has served as president of the American Psychology Association's division of educational psychology and the American Educational Research Association. He has a Ph.D. in educational psychology from Stanford University and has taught at California State University at San Jose, the University of Massachusetts, and the University of Arizona.

MYRNA S. COONEY is a teacher with over 35 years of classroom experience. She currently teaches grades 6 and 7 at the Taft Middle School in Cedar Rapids, Iowa, and serves on curriculum committees for language arts and social studies. She has previously taught grades 4, 5, and 6 at Cleveland Elementary School in Cedar Rapids. Ms. Cooney has a B.A. in education from Coe College and an M.A. in education from the University of Iowa. She has been an instructor in a teacher-in-service program at the University of Iowa and a teacher-in-residence at Vanderbilt University.

M. SUZANNE DONOVAN (Study Director) is a senior program officer at the National Research Council's Commission on Behavioral and Social Sciences and Education and study director for the Committee on Minority Representation in Special Education. Her interests span issues of education and public policy. She has a Ph.D. from the University of California, Berkeley, School of Public Policy and was previously on the faculty of Columbia University's School of Public and International Affairs.

ARTHUR EISENKRAFT is the science coordinatory (grades 6-12) and physics teacher in the Bedford Public Schools in Bedford, New York. He has taught high school physics in a variety of schools for 24 years. Dr. Eisenkraft is currently on the Interstate New Teacher Assessment and Support Consortium Science Standards Drafting Committee, and on the National Research Council's Advisory Panel to the Center for Science, Mathematics and Engineering Education. He is the editor and project manager of the National Science Foundation-supported Active Physics Curriculum Project of the American Institute of Physics and the American Association of Physics Teachers. His many publications include a lab text on laser applications, an audiotape history of the discovery of nuclear fission, middle school and high school curriculum materials, and numerous audiovisual productions. He holds a U.S. patent for a laser vision testing system. Dr. Eisenkraft serves on several science award committees and has served as executive director for the International Physics Olympiad. He has a Ph.D. in science education from New York University and received the Presidential Award for Excellence in Science Teaching in 1986.

HERBERT P. GINSBURG is the Jacob H. Schiff foundation professor of psychology and education at Teachers College, Columbia University. His work focuses on the intellectual development and education of young children, particularly poor and minority children. He has conducted research on the development of mathematical thinking and cognition in children, examining the implications for instruction and assessment in early education. His many publications include *The Development of Mathematical Thinking* (1983), *Piaget's Theory of Intellectual Development* (1988), *Children's Arithmetic* (1989), *Entering the Child's Mind: The Clinical Interview in Psychological Research and Practice* (1997), and *The Teacher's Guide to Flexible Interviewing in the Classroom* (1998). Dr. Ginsburg currently serves on the National Research Council's Committee on Early Childhood Pedagogy and on the Committee on Strategic Education Research Program Feasibility Study. He has a Ph.D. in developmental psychology from the University of North Carolina, Chapel Hill, and has taught at Cornell University, the University of Maryland, and the University of Rochester.

PAUL D. GOREN is the director of Child and Youth Development, Program on Human and Community Development, at the John D. and Catherine T. MacArthur Foundation. Previously, he was the executive director of policy and strategic services for the Minneapolis Public Schools and spent two years teaching middle school history and mathematics. He also worked as the director of the Education Policy Studies Division of the National Governors' Association, and as the coordinator of planning and research for the Stanford Teacher Education Program. He has a Ph.D. from the Stanford

University School of Education (1991) and an M.P.A. from the Lyndon B. Johnson School of Public Affairs at the University of Texas (1984).

JOSÉ P. MESTRE is a professor of physics and astronomy at the University of Massachusetts, Amherst. His research interests include cognitive studies of problem solving in physics, with a focus on the acquisition and use of knowledge by experts and novices. Most recently, his work has focused on applying research findings to the design of instructional strategies that promote active learning in large physics classes, and on developing physics curricula that promote conceptual development through problem solving. He is currently a member of the National Research Council's Committee on Developments in the Science of Learning and its Mathematical Sciences Education Board; the College Board's Sciences Advisory Committee, SAT Committee, and Council on Academic Affairs; the Educational Testing Service's Visiting Committee; the American Association of Physics Teacher's Research in Physics Education Committee and of the editorial board of *The Physics Teacher*, and the Federal Coordinating Council for Science, Engineering and Technology's Expert Panel. He has a Ph.D. in physics from the University of Massachusetts, Amherst.

ANNEMARIE SULLIVAN PALINCSAR holds a chair in the University of Michigan's School of Education, where she prepares teachers, teacher educators, and researchers to work in heterogeneous classrooms. She has conducted extensive research on peer collaboration in problem-solving activity, instruction to promote self-regulation, the development of literacy among learners with special needs, and the use of literacy across the school day. She is an editor of the books, *Strategic Teaching and Learning* and *Teaching Reading as Thinking*. Her cognition and instruction article on reciprocal teaching (co-authored with Ann Brown in 1984) is a classic. Dr. Palincsar currently serves on the National Research Council's Committee on the Prevention of Reading Difficulties in Young Children. She received an early contribution award from the American Psychological Association in 1988 and one from the American Educational Research Association in 1991. In 1992 she was elected a fellow by the International Academy for Research in Learning Disabilities. She has M.A. and Ph.D. degrees in special education from the University of Illinois at Urbana-Champaign.

ROY PEA is director of the Center for Technology in Learning at SRI International, in Menlo Park, California, and consulting professor in the School of Education at Stanford University. He also directs the multi-institutional Center for Innovative Learning Technologies, which aims to create a national knowledge network for catalyzing best practices and new designs for improving learning with technologies among researchers, schools, and industries. Previously, he was a John Evans professor of education and the learning sciences at Northwestern University, where he founded and chaired the learning sciences Ph.D. program and served as dean of the School of Education and Social Policy. He works as a cognitive scientist to integrate theory, research, and the design of effective learning environments using advanced technologies, with particular focus on science, mathematics, and technology. Dr. Pea currently serves on the National Research Council's Committee on Developments in the Science of Learning. He has a doctorate in developmental psychology from the University of Oxford, England, where he was a Rhodes scholar.